LIFE-CHANGING HABITS SERIES

YOUR PERSONAL BLUEPRINT FOR SUCCESS
AND HAPPINESS

THIBAUT MEURISSE

© 2017 Thibaut Meurisse

All rights reserved. No portion of this book may be reproduced in any form without permission from the publisher, except as permitted by U.S. copyright law.

PART I
GOAL SETTING
THE ULTIMATE GUIDE TO ACHIEVING LIFE CHANGING GOALS

What This Book is and Who It is For

You'll find many books on goal setting out there. Unfortunately, many fail to incorporate all the elements required for effective goal setting. They may focus on the mechanics of goal setting or teach you how to be more productive, but few provide you with all the pieces of the puzzle needed to ensure you'll achieve goals that genuinely excite you.

In this book, you'll discover the **SMARTEST Goal Method**, a comprehensive goal setting technique that encompasses all aspects of goal setting and will enable you to set and achieve goals you're genuinely excited about.

The SMARTEST Goal Method covers:

- How to overcome your limitations and unleash the power of your subconscious mind so you can achieve more than you ever thought possible
- How to set inspiring goals that deeply reflect your values and purpose
- How to avoid the seven deadly mistakes most people do when setting goals
- How to craft a clever strategy to maximize your chances of achieving your goals, and
- How to elaborate a clear plan of action you can use right away to work on your goals, and much more.

To ensure you get the most out of this book, I've also created a step-by-step workbook to guide you through the goal setting process. My aim is to remove any barriers that could prevent you from taking concrete action toward your goals and ambitions.

You'll greatly benefit from this book if:

- You want a clear step-by-step method to help you achieve your goals and aspirations
- You want to set and achieve exciting goals that reflect who you really are

- You don't want to settle, and you want more out of life.

If you recognized yourself in one of the cases above, this book is the right one for you.

So, if you are ready for the ride, let's get started.

Your Free Step-By-Step Workbook

Make sure you download your free workbook by entering the following URL in your browser:

http://whatispersonaldevelopment.org/life-changing-habits

If you have any difficulties downloading the workbook contact me at:

thibaut.meurisse@gmail.com

and I will send it to you as soon as possible.

How to Use This Book

To get the most out of this book, it's essential you use the workbook available at the end of this book. It's also crucial you commit to doing the exercises. This book is full of valuable information, but remember: how much you get out of the book is highly dependent upon how committed you are to carrying out its recommendations. The ball is in your court!

Feel free to re-read this book as often as necessary. Repetition is the key to mastery! See this book as a guide you can use to achieve any of your future goals.

If you have any questions, please email me at

thibaut.meurisse@gmail.com

You can also follow me on Facebook at

https://www.facebook.com/whatispersonaldevelopment.org/

I'm looking forward to hearing from you soon,

Thibaut Meurisse

Founder of Whatispersonaldevelopment.org

My author page:

http://amazon.com/author/thibautmeurisse

INTRODUCTION

 Mr. Rohn, let me see your current list of goals. I've had a lot of experience and I've been out here for a while, so let's go over them and maybe I can really give you some good ideas."

And I said, "I don't have a list."

He said, "Well, if you don't have a list of your goals, I can guess your bank balance within a few hundred dollars."

And he did.

— JIM ROHN, THE JIM ROHN GUIDE TO GOAL SETTING.

Thank you for purchasing this book. In doing so, you have already shown your commitment to bettering your life by setting goals that truly excite you. You have joined those who have made the decision to take more control over their lives and give less power to circumstances. It's important to think about where you want to be, whether it's one month, one year, or one decade from now. Taking the time to identify your destination is the best way to make sure you're going into the right direction. It will also prevent you from pursuing goals that won't fulfill you.

Deciding to set goals is probably one of the most important decisions you can make, but most people don't set clear goals in their life. It's almost as though they believe they have no control over their life and, as such, they wander through life heavily influenced by the circumstances and people surrounding them. These individuals give their power to their environments instead of using it to create the lives they desire. By doing this, they achieve far less than if they took the time to plan their lives and set specific goals.

Keep in mind, however, that simply having goals is not enough. In fact, having goals that are unclear or out of alignment with what you want, can be almost as bad as having none at all. Unfortunately, many goal setters spend years in dogged pursuit of a particular goal, only to achieve it, and then realize it isn't what they genuinely wanted. This book will help you avoid this situation.

Setting specific goals is one of the best decisions I've made in my life, and the information within this book will give you an opportunity to do the same.

I first created a list of goals back in September 2014 while in the process of building my website. Looking back, I often wonder why I'd never done it before, and why I never learned about it in school. However, setting goals is essential when it comes to personal development..

I believe we all have the potential to accomplish great things in life. However, many of us never learned to tap into our intrinsic ability to self-motivate. We spend our childhoods studying to reach good grades and trying to 'conform', in an attempt to please our parents, teachers, or our peers. We then spend our adulthoods working for money and other external motivators, which are also called 'outside' or 'extrinsic' motivators.

Our tendency to rely upon external motivators is ironic considering how ineffective they are. Studies show that external motivators, such as money or praise, are less efficient than internal motivators like autonomy, mastery, or purpose. Autonomy is our desire to direct our own lives and have more freedom when working on a project. Mastery is our desire to get better, to master something just because we feel good about ourselves. Purpose is our desire to partake in something that is bigger than ourselves.

The carrot and stick approach is still in frequent use these days, but it's far from ideal, and not always successful in the longer term. In reality, internal motivation yields better results and provides a greater sense of fulfillment than external motivation does.

Fortunately, learning to set the right goals will help you tap into your intrinsic motivation and allow you to uncover your hidden potential.

This book will help you define your goals and the kind of life you want to create for yourself. It will help you set goals that inspire you, stir your soul, and make you want to jump out of bed every morning. Goal setting might seem intimidating at first, but trust me, the journey is more than worth it in the long run!

1
WHY GOAL SETTING IS IMPORTANT

> *People without goals are doomed to work forever for people who do have goals.*
>
> — BRIAN TRACY, AUTHOR AND MOTIVATIONAL SPEAKER.

Setting Goals Gives Direction to your Subconscious Mind

> *Your automatic creative mechanism is teleological. That is, it operates in terms of goals and end results. Once you give it a definite goal to achieve, you can depend upon its automatic guidance system to take you to that goal much better than "you" ever could by conscious thought. "You" supply the goal by thinking in terms of end results. Your automatic mechanism them supplies the means whereby.*
>
> — MAXWELL MALTZ, AUTHOR OF PSYCHO-CYBERNETICS.

Did you know your subconscious mind can help you achieve your goal? Setting goals gives you a direction in life, but vague goals, like making more money or being happy, won't lead to a fulfilling life.

Your unconscious mind is like a powerful machine, and understanding how it works is a big part of successful goal setting. Hypnotherapist Joseph Clough compares it to a GPS, whereas Maxwell Maltz, author of Psycho-Cybernetics, calls it a mechanical goal-seeking device. Consider it this way. If you give your GPS an address, it will do whatever it can to point you to your destination. The subconscious mind behaves similarly. Have you ever learned a new word only to find yourself hearing it everywhere you go? This is an example of your brain 'priming.' In other words, your subconscious mind is scanning your environment for all information relevant to the word, phrase, or details you've given it. This is why setting clear goals gives you a greater chance to accomplish them. This sends a strong signal to your subconscious mind, which allows it to unleash its focusing power and look for any opportunity to achieve the goal. I will talk more about the importance of setting specific goals later in this book.

Setting Goals Empowers You

If you don't design your own life plan, chances are you'll fall into someone else's plan. And guess what they have planned for you? Not much.

— JIM ROHN, AUTHOR AND MOTIVATIONAL SPEAKER.

Are you the one choosing your goals? Or are others choosing them for you? When you start setting your own goals in all major areas of your life, you stop giving your power away.

When you start setting goals in all major areas of your life—your finances, your relationships, your career, your personal life, and your health—you stop giving power away and start empowering yourself. You make a conscious choice to become the creator of your own life and begin to take responsibility for every aspect of your life.

Imagine the difference it would make in your life if you took the time to figure out your goals for the future. If you knew how much you wanted to earn in five years, how long you wanted to live, and where you'd like to be in twenty years, what would you do differently?

Setting Goals Increases Self-Esteem

> *High self-esteem seeks the challenge and stimulation of worthwhile and demanding goals. Reaching such goals nurtures good self-esteem. Low self-esteem seeks the safety of the familiar and undemanding. Confining oneself to the familiar and undemanding serves to weaken self-esteem.*
>
> — NATHANIEL BRANDEN, AUTHOR OF THE SIX PILLARS OF SELF-ESTEEM.

Did you know you can increase your self-esteem by setting clear goals? It's worth mentioning that having clear goals and achieving them builds and reinforces our self-esteem. In fact, Nathaniel Branden (the author of "The Six Pillars of Self-Esteem") says part of our self-esteem comes from a 'disposition to experience ourselves as competent to cope with life's challenges.' With every goal we accomplish, we feel better equipped to deal with other goals and life challenges.

In his book, The Pursuit of Happiness, David G. Myers shows that high self-esteem is one of the best predictors of personal happiness. Consistently accomplishing the goals you set is one of the most efficient ways to build self-esteem.

Setting Goals Changes Your Reality

> *The value of goals is not in the future they describe, but the change in perception of reality they foster.*
>
> — DAVID ALLEN, AUTHOR OF GETTING THINGS DONE.

Setting goals is a valuable process for its own sake, regardless of whether or not you'll achieve them. You're probably wondering why that's the case. Well, there are several reasons. Goal setting helps you think about your future, gives you an opportunity to reflect on your values, and helps you discover what really matters to you. It will bring clarity and allow you to see the bigger picture of your life. It doesn't get much more valuable than this, I'd say.

Setting goals will also allow you to reconstruct your reality and realize dreams you previously thought unattainable are in fact achievable. It all starts with identifying your true goals, no matter how ambitious they are. This starts the process of overcoming your limiting beliefs, which stem from past experiences and make it harder to get the life you want. You'll soon realize how restrictive limiting beliefs are and just how many of them result from repetitive messages received from family, friends, and the media.

Lastly, goal setting will give you the opportunity to assess your current situation and will lead you to close the gap between where you are and where you want to be.

Setting Goals is Good for your Health

> *Use goals to live longer. No medicine in the world—and your physician will bear this out—is as powerful in bringing about life as is the desire to do something,*
>
> — DAVID J. SCHWARTZ, AUTHOR OF THE MAGIC OF THINKING BIG.

Dan Buettner, author of The Blue Zone: Lessons for Living Longer from the People Who've Lived the Longest, identified 'having a life purpose' as one of the nine characteristics shared by people who live to one hundred. Setting goals that really excite you is one of life's best medicines, and it will work wonders for your health. An alarming number of people die within a few years of retirement. One of the reasons for this, I believe, is they no longer have exciting goals to motivate them. This can be especially true for those who heavily identified with their job.

Still don't believe goals are good for your health? Check out the story of Miss D. from the book, The Magic of Thinking Big by David J. Schwartz:

> *Goals, intense goals, can keep a person alive when nothing else will. Mrs. D., the mother of a college friend of mine, contracted cancer when her son was only two. To darken matters, her husband had died only three months before her illness was diagnosed. Her physicians offered little hope. But Mrs. D. would not give up. She was determined to see her two-year-old son through college by operating a small retail store she inherited from her husband. She suffered numerous surgical operations. Each time the doctors would say, "Just a few more months." The cancer was never cured. But those "few more months" stretched into 20 years. She saw her son graduated from college. Six weeks later she was gone.*

What about you? Have you found goals that will motivate you well into old age? If not, read on.

* * *

Action step

Clarify *why* you want to set goals and *what* you want to get out of this book (*Section I. 1. Your expectations*)

* * *

2

HOW TO SET EXCITING GOALS

1. How to Choose the Right Goals

The main characteristics of worthy goals

> *We can say that an individual is healthy to the extent that the basic principle of motivation is that of motivation by confidence (love of self, love of life); the degree of motivation by fear is the measure of underdeveloped self-esteem.*
>
> — NATHANIEL BRANDEN, AUTHOR OF THE SIX PILLARS OF SELF-ESTEEM.

I believe worthy goals have the following features:

1. They reflect your core values and are what you want, not what friends, family, or society wants from you.
2. They truly excite and energize you.
3. You enjoy the process that leads to them and not just the final

outcome. "I'll be happy when..." types of goals are not goals worth pursuing. Why not be happy now?

To discern whether you're acting out of fear or love, you must closely examine your focus. **When you act out of love, your main focus is on giving. When you act out of fear, your main focus is on receiving something, be it money, approval, recognition, fame, or power.**

Acting out of love means you aren't trying to get people to like you, rather, you just want them to be happy. If you act out of love, the feeling of helping people, while doing what you love, will make you happy.

The desire to be famous, obtain money, or gain power can certainly motivate people to reach their goals, but people with such motivations are acting out of fear. They're trying to fill the emptiness within them through external recognition. I suggest, such goals are not truly worthy ones. In fact, they reflect a sense of insecurity and a lack of self-esteem, which is the very reason some seemingly successful people aren't happy. External things like money or fame never lead to true fulfillment. As Jim Carrey says, "I wish everyone could get rich and famous and have everything they ever dreamed of so they would know that's not the answer."

If your motives are external, ponder the following questions:

1. Do you feel as if you aren't good enough?
2. Are you trying to prove something to yourself or others?
3. What are you trying to achieve with your goal?

Acting out of love isn't easy and requires a great deal of personal development. You have to ask yourself frequently whether you're acting out of love or fear. You need to make a conscious effort to focus on helping others and personal fulfillment, rather than making money or gaining recognition.

Worthy vs. unworthy goals

An example of an unworthy goal is going into a field you have no interest in just because you think you can make a lot of money. This isn't a worthy goal. More often than not, you won't end up making much money if you don't like what you're doing. Identifying an unworthy goal is easier than you think. An unworthy goal won't reflect your values, nor will it excite you. The process of achieving it won't be enjoyable, and it won't involve giving to others, or acting out of love.

An example of a worthy goal would be going into a business you love, one that allows you to live by your deepest values. These values could be freedom, connection or contribution (see examples below). Either way, a worthy goal will stem from a sincere desire to make a difference in people's lives.

A worthy goal will reflect your values and excite you. The process of achieving it will be enjoyable, and it will involve both giving and acting out of love.

There's no guarantee you'll make a lot of money, but in the second case, you'll at least enjoy the process. Your goal will give you meaning. You're also more likely to persevere for a longer period due to your passion and genuine desire to contribute.

Below are some examples of values

Freedom is:

- Wanting to have a flexible schedule
- Wanting to work from home, and
- Wanting to travel regularly.

Connection is:

- Wanting to work in team most of the day, and
- Wanting to meet new people.

Contribution is:

- Wanting to feel you're making an impact on people's lives.

While we all aspire for freedom, connection and contribution, the degree will vary from one person to another as shown below:

- Freedom: some people may have a strong need to work on their own with a flexible schedule, while for other people the need for connecting with others or security, might be more important.
- Connection: an extrovert may have a stronger need for connection than an introvert.
- Contribution: Some people may need to feel the direct impact of their work on people's lives, while others may find greater pleasure in mastering their work independently of the impact they're making.

Questions to Consider:

Are you acting out of fear? If so, what does this tell about your self-esteem and the worthiness of your goal? What can you do about it?

The main pitfalls to avoid when setting goals

When properly done, setting goals empowers you. Even so, if you aren't careful, you might experience some obstacles. Now, I'm going to outline a few pitfalls so that you can avoid them. If you take these potential issues into consideration before setting goals, you'll be better equipped to face them successfully.

1. Being unaware of limiting factors

Our brain is wired to seek rewards and avoid pain, discomfort, and fear. It's not wired for change, so watch out for fear of failure. It can lead to self-sabotage if you don't keep it in check. You'll also have to identify any limiting beliefs or mental blocks that may hold you back.

Solution:

Become aware of, manage, and eradicate limiting beliefs. (I'll have more on that in the section "Transferring Your Goals to the Subconscious.")

2. Focusing excessively on your goal

This involves becoming so focused on your goal that you neglect other aspects of your life.

Solution: Be sure to reevaluate your goal on a regular basis and assess how it fits in your life as a whole.

3. Going too big

In an article entitled, "*The Hazards of Goal Pursuit,*" L.A. King and C.M. Burton argue that we should only use goals in the narrowest of circumstances. Their article states that,

> *The optimally striving individual ought to endeavor to achieve and approach goals that only slightly implicate the self; that are only moderately important, fairly easy, and moderately abstract; that do not conflict with each other, and that concern the accomplishment of something other than financial gain.*

Solution: Break a big goal into smaller goals to avoid taking on something that is too overwhelming.

4. Neglecting the now

Focusing excessively on future goals can cause you to dwell on what you don't have rather than what you do have, which fuels the individual's tendency to want more and more. It's important to feel good when living in the present moment and not just when you think about your desires. There must be a balance, so it's crucial to have goals that improve your present reality and accurately reflect your core values, rather than goals you can only enjoy in the future.

Solution: Using visualization every day to make you feel good about having that new house or car you desire is great, but isn't there more to life than this? Think about it and make sure you enjoy the present moment as well.

5. Getting too specific

Specific goals aren't bad, but they may keep you from seeing your overall progress. If you missed your weight loss goal by five pounds or accomplished something a week later than intended, for instance, you might believe the illusory notion you've failed. In reality, however, success and failure aren't so black and white. The primary function of goals is to ensure you live in alignment with your core values—they aren't supposed to make you beat yourself up.

Solution: Ensure your goals align with who you are and don't fixate on minor details. If you're unable to accomplish every aspect of your goal, congratulate yourself for the parts you did accomplish, and remember your 'why.' Missing some minor targets isn't the end of the world, and plenty of other doors will open as you continue the journey towards your major goal.

Also, make sure you focus on the process (what you do every day) and stay consistent. You have limited control over the outcome of your actions, but you have 100% control over the actions you take every day to move closer to your goal. We'll talk about the importance of having daily habits later in this book.

6. Having too many goals

Often, people fail to achieve their goals because they have too many of them. As a result, their effort and attention becomes diluted, preventing them from gaining tangible results with their goals.

Solution: Focus only on a limited number of goals at a time. Make a note of the other projects you'd like to work on and jot down ideas when necessary, but don't start working on them until you complete some of your current goals. You might want to schedule these goals for a later date.

7. Being a victim of the shiny object syndrome

Many people fail to achieve their goals because they keep jumping from one thing to another, never learning to stick to a goal long enough to accomplish it.

Solution: Avoid jumping from one course to another or one diet to the next. Instead, do your research, find something that works for you, and stick to it until you master the process. Eventually, you'll reach your goal. Set a few major goals and refocus on them whenever you feel overwhelmed or catch yourself doing too many unrelated things.

* * *

Action step

Answer the questions in the workbook to shed light on some of the mistakes you make when setting goals. (*Section II. Setting Exciting goals - 1. How to choose the right goals - a. Setting worthy goals, and b. Avoiding Pitfalls.*)

* * *

For more in-depth information regarding the process-focused approach, check out my advanced goal setting book, *The One Goal, Master the Art of Goal Setting, Win Your Inner Battles, and Achieve Exceptional Results.*

2. How to Set Inspiring Goals

> *The key to goal setting is for you to think on paper. Successful men and women think with a pen in their hands; unsuccessful people do not.*
>
> — BRIAN TRACY, AUTHOR AND MOTIVATIONAL SPEAKER.

If you want to set goals, you should first put them on paper. The act of writing them down using pen and paper will instantly make them more concrete in your mind. It's as though putting goals on paper moves the things you daydream about from the abstract world to the physical world. Daydreaming feels good in the moment, but it's just an illusion.

Once you take the time to write down your goals, however, they start to become part of your reality.

A Simple Yet Powerful Goal Setting Exercise:

 Setting goals is the first step in turning the invisible into the visible.

— TONY ROBBINS, AUTHOR, ENTREPRENEUR AND LIFE COACH.

I'm going to share with you one of the most powerful exercise to set goals. Make sure you download the free workbook at http://whatispersonaldevelopment.org/goal-setting-workbook and follow the instructions (or use the workbook at the end of this book).

This exercise is very simple. All you have to do is **write down all the goals you would like to achieve if you were guaranteed to succeed no matter what.**

Focus on goals that really excite you, even if they sound totally crazy to others. What is it *you* really want? What *your* dream life would look like? What is *your* way to contribute to the world? Unleash your imagination!

I was talking to a friend recently and asked her if she had any dreams. She said no, but I had a feeling this wasn't true and asked again. I'm sure you can imagine my face when she suddenly said, "I want to change the world!"

"That's great! I want to change the world too," I replied. "The question is how are you going to do it? What is your unique way to change the world?"

She explained to me she thought her dream was too big. She said she would be happy if she could do something to change the world, even if it was something tiny. Like many other people, she wouldn't allow herself to dream big, but it's important to do so. You must allow yourself to dream big!

Whatever you do, **don't limit yourself in any way** while doing this exercise. Forget the excuses or limitations for a while and pretend you're playing a game. Make sure you're in a constructive state of mind. You can listen to your favorite song or whatever else elevates your mood. Take your time, do the exercise now, and ask yourself: What is it I want?

This process is crucial. It's unlikely you'll get much from this book if you skip it. So, go ahead and try it. Don't worry I'll wait.

All done? Great! How was it? How many inspiring goals did you come up with? How do they make you feel?

Now, here is the funny part. I want you to ask yourself this simple, yet powerful question: *How?* How are you going to achieve these big goals? If it helps, you can imagine you'll be beaten with birch twigs if you don't achieve them. Refrain from using limiting phrases such as 'I can't,' or 'It's impossible.' Ban these words and phrases from your vocabulary, and try to enjoy yourself, as you consider how you'll achieve what you want to accomplish. **Take at least ten minutes to brainstorm**, but you should only focus on your most important goal for now. You can think about the others later on.

Okay, now you've written down your goals and brainstormed how to achieve the most important one. How did this feel?

Next, I want you to ask yourself, **"What is one tiny step, if taken today, would get me closer to my goal?"** Once you've figured it out, take this tiny step today! It doesn't matter how small it is. It might entail sending a message to someone, buying a book, doing some Internet research, calling a friend, or going to a particular location. The particular action or activity isn't important—getting started is what counts.

I want you to remember this simple truth: **Every goal, regardless of its size, can be achieved through a succession of tiny steps taken every day.** The more you break your goal into manageable tasks, the easier it'll be to achieve. By taking small steps every day, you'll start building momentum and, therefore, continue to take action. Goals that once seemed impossible, will begin to appear achievable. You'll also avoid the pressure that comes when you try to deal with huge goals, which in turn, reduces the potential for self-sabotage. We'll discuss how to break down your goals in the section "Chunking down your goals."

* * *

Action step

Use the workbook to do the goal setting exercise mentioned above.

- Write down what you really want. (*Section II. - 2a. What do you really want?*)
- Write down how you're going to get there. (*Section II - 2b. How are you going to get there?*)
- Write down your very first step. (*Section II. - 2c. What is my first step?*)

* * *

3. How to Align Your Goal with Your Values

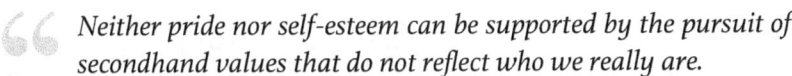 *Neither pride nor self-esteem can be supported by the pursuit of secondhand values that do not reflect who we really are.*

— NATHANIEL BRANDEN, AUTHOR OF THE SIX PILLARS OF SELF-ESTEEM.

It's imperative your goal is in line with your core values. If the goal you are pursuing is not in line with your core values and doesn't excite you, you are unlikely to achieve it. If you don't have a strong 'why' to support your goal, it will be hard to cope with the obstacles and failures you'll experience on your way to achieving it. You may even find it impossible to reach.

Identifying the values behind your goals

Understanding the deepest motivations behind your goal will make you feel good about what you wish to achieve, and will provide more reason to persevere when things become difficult.

So, take your biggest goal and ask yourself why it's important to you.

What are all the values you attach to this particular goal? If your goal is to make a certain amount of money, figure out what values you attach to money.

In this section, I will share with you an exercise from hypnotherapist Joseph Clough that will help you not only identify the values you attached to your goals, but also supercharge them.

But, before we get started, as a warm-up exercise, I would like you to write your answers to the following questions using your workbook or a pen and a piece of paper:

- Why do you want to achieve this specific goal?
- What emotional benefit do you expect to gain by achieving it?

Don't overthink it, just write down the first thing that comes to mind. We'll be using your answers to complete the exercise.

Now, here is the exercise from hypnotherapist Joseph Clough:

1. Take a pen and a piece of paper and write down one specific goal you want to accomplish. I recommend you use the goal you've selected during the previous exercise.
2. Write down what values you'll get from achieving this particular goal
3. For each value go deeper by asking yourself why it's important to you (see example below).

To give you a specific example, here's a look at what I wrote when I applied this exercise to my most important goal (which is having a successful blog that generates 100,000 page views per month). I asked myself what achieving this goal would give me, and I discovered it would provide:

Fulfillment as a result of helping people

- Happiness

- Enhanced Self-Esteem

- Stronger sense of purpose

A passive income

- More freedom:

  - Self-employment/independence
  - An end to my daily commute
  - The means of doing what I love
  - The means to decide my own schedule

- Extra time to:

  - Write more books and articles
  - Study coaching, hypnosis or psychology
  - Improve my public speaking skills
  - Start new, exciting projects

- Better health:

  - The ability to take a rest when I need to, and
  - Less stress as a result of loving what I do.

This is just one example, of course, and you should fill in the exercise with whatever applies to you. The point is to go deeper and deeper into the benefits that your most important goals will bring you to create a stronger "why". **You can make any goal more meaningful by taking the time to think about the ways in which it will impact your life.** Go beyond the superficial. Think about how the goal will impact your health, mood, self-esteem, relationships, career, and any other important aspects of your life.

Now it's your turn! What is exciting about your goal? What benefits will you get from achieving it? Complete this exercise on the downloadable workbook (3a. What would achieving my goal get me?) and make your goal as exciting and inspiring as you can.

* * *

Action step

Use the workbook to write down what you'd get from achieving your goal. (*Section II. 3a. What would achieving my goal get me?*)

* * *

4. How to Align Your Goal with Your Life Purpose

Life purpose vs. ideal goal

Now you know your most important goal, you should ask yourself, "What is the value of this goal?" **Remember, a goal is only valuable when the meaning we give it provides us with fulfillment.** Your goal is only one of several ways you can achieve the sense of fulfillment you're looking for, and it's important not to confuse your goal with your life purpose.

For instance, my life purpose is to, "Improve myself every day in order to live up to my full potential, and help others realize their true potential, so they can live happier, more fulfilling lives."

For me, realizing my life purpose was transformative. I was shy and passive most of my life, but eventually realized I wouldn't achieve my goals unless I started taking action. Without changing, I would reach my deathbed full of regret for not living the life I was supposed to, and for not having had the impact upon society I should have done. I didn't want such an ending, so I embarked on a journey of personal development that allowed me to come progressively out of my shell. I discovered I wanted to study, learn, evolve, and improve myself for the rest of my life. If I could work on myself, become more confident, and take more action, I could help others do the same. The main reason I've been able to start a blog, write a number of books, and shoot videos, is because these things are in sync with my values, and with what I want to get out of life. If it didn't motivate me, I wouldn't have the courage to follow through, leave my comfort zone, and keep moving forward despite challenges.

Having a life purpose is without a doubt what motivated me to take action.

The idea of unleashing potential is also important to me because of the people I've watched miss out on their dreams. I have relatives who could have achieved much more in life, had they been able to overcome their lack of confidence, fear of failure, or limiting beliefs. Furthermore, I feel most people greatly underestimate their potential to accomplish great things in their lives.

My ultimate goal stems from my life purpose and has three parts. I want to become one of the best personal development experts, run a successful blog and write books that help people unleash their true potential. I could easily be overwhelmed by such an ambitious goal. However, this goal is *not* my life purpose. **If what I'm doing is in line with my life purpose, I will be satisfied even if I fail to achieve that goal.** I will feel fulfilled as long as I have a career that allows me to evolve and help others grow and maximize their potential. There is more than one way to do this, such as coaching or teaching, which may or may not involve achieving my ultimate goal.

Identifying the values behind a specific goal as we did in the previous exercise, opens us up to new possibilities and gives us more flexibility to adapt our goals to ensure they reflect our values. My goal of reaching at least 100,000 page views per month has no meaning in itself, the freedom and sense of accomplishment it will give me is what's important. Reaching 50,000 page views per month might generate enough passive income to allow me to live from my passion, while touching enough people's lives to provide the sense of contribution I seek.

Or perhaps having a few thousand loyal subscribers would generate the same results.

Setting an ambitious goal is still beneficial, however. In my specific case, it motivates me to do more and to give as much as I can to my readers. Setting your own ambitious goal can have a similarly motivational effect on you.

Identifying your life purpose

Knowing your core values and having a strong life purpose are vital components of having a life that is truly fulfilling. Unfortunately, many people will spend their entire lives pursuing worthless goals because they have no sense of purpose. **Most people lack a sense of purpose because they don't know themselves.** These individuals have been trying so hard to meet the expectations of their friends, parents, and societal expectations they haven't learned to listen to themselves. It's difficult to discover your life purpose if you don't know your core values, which is why it's crucial to spend time getting to know yourself.

To reach the essence of who you are, you must take steps to eliminate your limiting beliefs and deconstruct the false reality that was created by your environment. Otherwise, you risk coming up with a life purpose that's mostly the product of external influences. Remember this, because you cannot accept anything out of alignment with your belief system, the life purpose you discover will always be a reflection of your own subjective reality. As such, it may be necessary to change your belief system before you can find your true purpose. Discovering your life purpose will allow you to unleash your potential and, by doing so, work won't feel like work anymore. As Confucius said, "Choose a job you love, and you will never have to work a day in your life."

Finding your life purpose might take some time. Be patient and learn to listen to your emotions. Identify what you are passionate about and see what this says about your values. **Once you've discovered your true passion, commit to it, take action, and persevere.** When you do this, it will be very hard for people or circumstances to stop you!

The characteristics of a great life purpose

To further help you, let me give you the main characteristics of a great life purpose. A great life purpose should be:

1. **Timeless:** If you could use a time travel machine and go back in time or travel to the future, your life purpose would remain the same.

2. **Universal:** If you were born in a different part of the world your purpose would still be the same.
3. **Inspiring:** Your life purpose should be truly inspiring, allowing you to unleash your full potential, and enabling you to experience a real sense of fulfillment. When your purpose resonates within you, what you're doing doesn't feel like work.
4. **Transcendent:** Your life purpose should help you transcend your fears and insecurities. Most people seek to gain recognition or feel accepted by society. These are fear-based motivators. **A genuine life purpose should encourage you to act from a place of love, not fear.**

3 practical exercises to discover your life purpose

Now, let me give you some exercises to help you discover your life purpose.

Exercise 1:

Take the most important goal you identified during the goal setting exercise. This goal in itself could certainly be a way for you to express your life purpose. What are the values behind this goal? Take some time to think about these values and try to connect them with a possible life purpose.

Exercise 2:

Ask yourself the following questions:

- If I had all the money and time in the world what would I do? - This question removes any sense of limitation and allows you to go wild.
- What do I love so much that I'd pay to do it? - This question helps you find out what you really love to do.
- How can I get paid to do what I love to do? - This question allows you to brainstorm potential ideas to help you design your dream career.
- Who do I envy? - When you envy other people, it's usually

because they have something you want. As such, this question can help you discover what you really want to do.

Exercise 3:

Take a pen and a piece of paper and answer the following question: "What is my life purpose?" Don't overthink it, just write whatever comes to mind. Keep doing it until the sentence you write makes you cry.

This exercise is originally from Steve Pavlina's article, *How to Discover Your Life Purpose in About 20 Minutes*. For more information type, "How to discover your life purpose in about 20 minutes" in your favorite search engine.

To learn how to uncover your passion and make a living from it check out *The Passion Manifesto: Escape the Rat Race, Uncover Your Passion and Design a Career and Live You Love*

* * *

Action step

Complete some or all of the three exercises above using the workbook. (*Section II. 4a. Discovering my life purpose.*)

* * *

3

SETTING SMARTEST GOALS

> *As long as you are alive, you'll either live to accomplish your own goals and dreams, or you'll be used as a resource to accomplish someone else's goals and dreams.*
>
> — GRANT CARDONE, AUTHOR AND MOTIVATIONAL SPEAKER

Now we've discussed how to set exciting goals that are in line with your values and life purpose, we're going to delve more deeply into the goal setting process. In this section, you'll learn how to set goals effectively using the **SMARTEST Goals Method**.

More specifically, you'll learn:

- How to set specific, measurable goals you'll actually achieve
- How to prepare yourself mentally, develop great perseverance, and achieve your goals
- How to strategize effectively to maximize your chances of reaching your goals
- How to chunk down your goals and schedule tasks effectively, and
- How to reprogram your mind to overcome limiting beliefs.

SMART Goals Method

You may have heard about SMART goals before, but it's worth reviewing what they are before we delve into the SMARTEST Goals Method.

SMART stands for:

- **Specific:** you know exactly what your goal is.
- **Measurable:** you can measure and track your goal.
- **Achievable:** your goal is realistic (i.e. you believe you can achieve it).
- **Relevant:** your goal is relevant to you (i.e. it is exciting and meaningful).
- **Time-bound:** you have a clear deadline for your goal.

SMART goals are effective, but, when it comes to setting and achieving goals, it's just one part of a bigger picture. The SMART method focuses solely on technical issues, and overlooks psychological issues such as your belief system, your mental preparation, and the overall strategic planning needed to achieve your goal. For this reason, I recommend using the **SMARTEST Goals Method** instead.

SMARTEST goals build upon SMART goals and offer a more comprehensive approach to goal setting.

The SMARTEST Goals Method

SMARTEST stands for:

- **Specific:** What exactly do you want? What are you trying to achieve?
- **Measurable:** Can you assess the progress towards your goal easily? How will you know whether you've achieved it?
- **Achievable:** Is it achievable? Is the timeframe realistic? Can you put in the effort required despite other responsibilities?
- **Relevant:** Is it in line with your values? Is it exciting you?
- **Time-bound:** Do you have a clear deadline for your goals?
- **Emotionally Sustainable:** Are you mentally prepared for the

obstacles you'll encounter during the journey towards your goal? Learning to persevere is vital to your success!
- Strategized: Do you know exactly how you're going to reach your goals? Do you know the key factors for your success? What skills must you master? How must you prioritize your actions to reach your goal?
- Transfer goals to the Subconscious: Most of us have limiting beliefs, many of which may be subconscious. You must take eliminating these limiting beliefs **very** seriously. Otherwise, they might prevent you reaching your goal.

From now on, we'll set goals that follow the **SMARTEST Goals Method**. We won't mention the "R" (relevant), which refers to the "why" behind your goals. We already covered this in the first part of this book when we addressed your core values and life purpose. We'll cover the following:

- Making your goal specific (S)
- Having measurable goals (M)
- Setting goals that are achievable (A)
- *(Setting exciting, relevant goals - covered in part I (R)*
- Having a clear deadline (T)
- Having an emotionally sustainable goal (E)
- Strategizing your goal (S)
- Transferring your goal to the subconscious (T)

1. Making Your Goal Specific (S)

> *Know what you want. Clarity is power. And vague goals promote vague results.*
>
> — ROBIN SHARMA, AUTHOR AND LEADERSHIP SPEAKER.

By now, you should have a clear idea of the values behind your goal. The next step is to ensure your goal is as specific as possible. Your mind likes clarity, and having clear goals will drive you to take action. It's almost impossible to move forward with vague goals.

An example of clarity's power

For a deeper understanding of clarity's importance, let's do a quick exercise from the book *Made to Stick* by Chip and Dan Heath:

Take fifteen seconds to list as many white things as you can. How many things could you think of?

Now take fifteen seconds to list as many white things in your refrigerator as you can.

* * *

Action step

Use the workbook to do the exercise now. I'll wait for you and give you my own answers. (*Section III. 1a. The power of clarity.*)

My answers:

- For the first question, I came up with things like Apple computers and snow.
- For the second question, some of the things I came up with were eggs, tofu, salad dressing, and the fridge itself. Most people can list as many white things in their refrigerators as they can in the entire world!

This exercise goes to show that specific goals allow you to tap into the focusing power of your mind. Vague goals do not, so your mind won't be able to support you in achieving them.

* * *

Clarifying your goals

The truth is most people never learn to clarify their goals. Last December, I asked a friend if he had any goals for the New Year, to which he replied he wanted to study Japanese and eat more healthily. Unfortunately, those are not goals. They're merely imprecise ideas.

The clearer version of my friend's goal to study Japanese might be something along the lines of, "I will study Japanese 30 minutes every day right after I take a shower." He would then need to decide what exactly he's aiming for and in what timeframe. He might decide he wants to be able to have a conversation in Japanese, write 500 Kanji (Chinese characters), or read a certain book in Japanese by the end of the year.

The goal to eat healthier food is as vague as the goal to study Japanese, but you could clarify it in the following ways:

1. I will eat at least five servings of vegetables every day.
2. I will refrain from eating sugar on Mondays and Thursdays except for fruit.
3. I will change from white to brown rice.

As you can see, it's much easier to act on your goals when you have a concrete plan and put it in writing. You'll know when you stray from the plan, and you can assess your progress more easily. Your goals will also be more tangible and easier to visualize, which sends a powerful signal to your mind regarding where its focus should be.

The bottom line is this: The more you clarify your goal, the more likely you are to achieve it.

Key Lessons:

Your goal should be specific. You should know exactly what you want to achieve and what you need to do to accomplish it.

* * *

Action step

Make your goal as specific as possible using the workbook. (*Section III. 1b. Clarifying your goal.*)

* * *

2. Having measurable goals (M)

 What gets measured, gets done.

— Peter Drucker, management consultant and author.

It's essential your goal be measurable. Otherwise, how will you keep track of your progress and adjust your efforts and strategies over time? And how will you know whether you've achieved it?

Some goals are easier to measure than others. For instance, "I'll earn $5,000 per month by the end of the year" is pretty straightforward. Either you're making $5,000 or you aren't. This would be the same for the weight you want to lose, or the pounds of muscle you want to gain.

In other situations, making your goal measurable might be quite challenging. Our previous example, "I want to learn Japanese", would be one of these scenarios. With goals that can't be easily quantified, we must come up with our own qualitative criteria to measure our progress. For instance, "Having a conversation around travel with my Japanese friend," could be measured to a certain degree. Either you can talk about travel in Japanese or you can't. However, it's still insufficient and would have to be further defined by establishing specific criteria. Think of the way judges evaluate speeches or sports performances. They have a notation system. It's not perfect, but it ensures a certain degree of fairness when assessing participants performances. A similar system is necessary for qualitative goals.

What about you? How will you measure your goal?

Setting your KPIs

Key Performance Indicators (KPI) are indicators used in business to measure the performance of companies, departments within companies, and even employees. KPIs can also be applied to personal goals. If you want to write a book, the number of pages you write per day, week or month would be a KPI. Another KPI could be how many words you write per hour. If you can only dedicate 30 minutes per day, 5 days a week to your goal, and plan to write a 200-page book in a year, you would need to write an average of 0.77 pages per day (200 / 5 x 52 weeks = 0.77 pages/day). One page is about 250 words, so you'd need to write an average of 192.5 words per day. Assuming 30 minutes of work per day, that would require writing less than 400 words per hour which is more than doable. Of course, you would need to factor in time for editing, research, and other activities as well.

Setting a clear KPI of 200 words per day and assessing your progress on a weekly and monthly basis would ensure you stay on track with your goal and achieve it within the set timeframe.

For the goal of studying Japanese, it could be the amount of time spent studying each day, or counting the increase in your vocabulary.

What KPIs could you set to help you achieve your goals?

Key Lessons:

You don't know whether you've achieved a goal until you have a specific way to measure it. Make sure:

- Your goal can be measured (so you should know whether you've achieved it or not)
- It can be measured using quality measurements that are effective (for a non-quantifiable goal)
- You use KPIs to track the progress you make on your goal (words written per day, for instance)

* * *

Action step

- Use the workbook to write down your goal while ensuring that it's measurable. (*Section III. 2a. Having measurable goals.*)
- Set KPIs for your goal. (*Section III. 2b. Setting your own KPIs.*)

* * *

3. Setting Goals That are Achievable (A)

Setting a realistic goal

 There are no unrealistic goals, only unrealistic timeframes.

— Jack Canfield, motivational speaker and co-author of the Chicken Soup for the Soul series.

Gauging the feasibility of your goals can be tricky. When trying to discern whether your goal is realistic, it's best to use your feelings. Does it feel like you're struggling? Are you overwhelmed and frequently doubting your ability to achieve your goal? If so, you need to break the goal down into smaller steps.

Be honest with yourself regarding how you feel about your goal. If it doesn't sound realistic under the current timeframe, change the timeframe or break the goal down into smaller steps until you feel confident you can achieve it. Attaining your goal should be challenging enough to push you out of your comfort zone, but it shouldn't encourage self-sabotage or make you feel overwhelmed and discouraged.

For instance, as I mentioned before, my ultimate goal is to increase the traffic of my website at least 100,000 page views per month. I could easily become discouraged and ultimately give up if this was my only milestone. If I start small and focus on reaching 20,000 views per month over the course of 6 months, however, it sounds much more realistic.

If you don't believe that you can achieve a goal because it feels too big, you don't deserve it, or for any other reason, you'll struggle to achieve it. Worse yet, you're likely to engage in self-sabotage. This risk applies to conscious doubts as well as subconscious ones (there'll be more on that in the section "Emotionally Sustainable").

* * *

Action step

Assess how realistic your goal is by referring to the workbook. (*Section III. 3a. Setting realistic goals.*)

* * *

Chunking down your goal

As Henry Ford said, "Nothing is particularly hard if you break it down into small jobs." Your current goal may be extremely ambitious. But no matter how big it may be, you can always break it down into small, manageable tasks. It could be writing a page per day of the book you've always wanted to write. Or it could be studying fifteen minutes per day for the Japanese language test you want to take in a year or two. Or perhaps it's writing down all the tasks you need to complete for your side project and creating monthly, weekly, and daily objectives. As you can see, breaking your goals into 'bite size' chunks can be very beneficial. It allows you to avoid feeling overwhelmed and enables you to monitor your progress effectively.

Breaking down your goals and achieving small ones each and every day will also allow you to build momentum and gain confidence in your ability to achieve bigger goals. This, in turn, will boost your self-esteem.

Now, let's come back to the previous goal, "I want to study Japanese". Let's assume the main objective is to have a conversation in Japanese. For example's sake, we could further break it down as follows:

- By January 30th, I'll finish the first 10 lessons of my Japanese manual.
- By February 15th, I'll have a conversation in Japanese using the grammatical form and vocabulary introduced in the first 10 lessons of the manual.
- By February 28th, I'll complete all the lessons in my Japanese manual.
- By March 15th, I'll have a conversation with my Japanese friend in which I'll use all the grammatical points I've studied in the manual.
- By March 31st, I'll finish reading the Japanese book I bought the

other day and verbally summarize it in Japanese. I'll also prepare for some of the questions my friend may ask.
- By May 31st, I'll have a conversation with my Japanese friend about my experiences traveling in Asia.

These could be the main milestones for your goal of studying Japanese. Then, you would create weekly and daily goals. Maybe you would record yourself weekly using the grammatical form you've just learned. Or perhaps you would join a Japanese conversation group and make a conscious effort to apply what you learn in real life situations. These are just examples, of course, but you get the idea.

The bottom line is the more you can chunk down your goal and make your tasks manageable, the more likely you'll be to achieve them. Breaking your goal(s) down into manageable chunks allows you to:

- Define clearly what needs to be done to achieve your goal
- Set small, manageable tasks for each day or week, which prevents you from feeling overwhelmed
- Boost your self-esteem as you set and achieve small goals one after the another, and
- Build more momentum as you work on your goal every day.

* * *

Action step

Use the workbook to break your goal into monthly, weekly, and daily goals. *(Section III. 3b. Chunking down your goal.)*

* * *

Going after big goals

 Don't set your goals too low. If you don't need much, you won't become much.

— JIM ROHN, AUTHOR AND MOTIVATIONAL SPEAKER.

On one hand, it's good to consider the feasibility of your goal. On the other hand, you want your ultimate goal to be something you truly want. You may wonder how big your goal should be. The answer to this question is: As big as you want it to be!

Setting big goals changes your outlook and perception almost instantly. It forces you to change your view of reality in order to find ways to reach your goals. You can't accomplish big things by setting small goals any more than you can accomplish a goal you haven't set or defined. Don't waste your time working towards something you don't genuinely want just because you think it's the best you can manage. Instead, create a big vision that genuinely excites you.

You might ask, "But what if my real goal doesn't seem remotely realistic to me right now?" and that's a perfectly normal reaction. If you earn $20,000 a year and your goal is to earn $1,000,000, it's logical your goal might sound unrealistic to you. This is where breaking your goals down into small, manageable steps comes in again. After all, a big goal is nothing more than a succession of hundreds or thousands of small goals achieved at regular intervals. When we look at successful people, we tend to see their accomplishments as something that came in big leaps. In most cases, however, this is an illusion. In reality, success starts with small steps and small gains.

So, remember it's the small steps you take every day that determines whether you'll achieve your goals, not the huge, hypothetical steps you may or may not take in the future. Get into the habit of working on your goals every day. You might tell yourself you'll do more tomorrow, but you probably won't. Always assume what you are doing today is what you'll be doing every day from now on. Then, ask yourself whether continuing to do what you've done today will enable you to achieve your big goal in the future.

As a side note, I don't recommend focusing too heavily on financial goals, but if you do, I would like to share this amazing Jim Rohn quote with you: "After you become a millionaire, you can give all your money away because what's important is not the million dollars; what's important is the person you have become in the process of becoming a millionaire." The point is: Don't forget to enjoy the process of personal growth. Try to see the creation of wealth as the result of personal development instead of your ultimate goal.

Wanting to become the best

Maybe your goal is to become the best in your field. In my view, there's nothing wrong with having such an ambitious goal. We should try to achieve as much as we can, and most of us are accomplishing far less than the best version of ourselves could. When we continually achieve less than we're capable of achieving, it's often due to the tremendous influence our environment has upon us. As motivational speaker Jim Rohn said, "You are the average of the five people you spend the most time with." If the people in your life don't make much money, for instance, it will be difficult to imagine earning five times more than they do. If, on the other hand, you have friends or relatives who are successful entrepreneurs, you would have higher limits regarding how much money it's possible to earn. Your environment plays a critical role in shaping your reality.

Even so, your environment doesn't have to determine how successful you will be--the mindset and limiting beliefs it created do this, but only if you allow it to happen.

Luckily, you have the power to change things. We have access to all the knowledge in the world through the Internet, and books have never been cheaper or easier to obtain. Your surroundings might be negative, but you can create a positive environment by reading things that are inspirational and by using positive affirmations each day. Your limiting beliefs formed through repetition. Therefore, you can overcome them through repetition, too.

If you overcome the limiting factors you can create a more empowering environment and keep growing until you become the type of person who can achieve your ambitious goals.

For more on that, refer to the section "Creating the Right Mindset" of this book. For an in-depth discussion of the topic, you might like to refer to my book *The One Goal: Master the Art of Goal Setting, Winn Your Inner Battles, and Achieve Exceptional Results*.

A final word about ambitious goals

If you have a particularly huge goal that few people can achieve (such as being a Hollywood star, for instance) make sure you identify the real "reason" behind it. What needs are you trying to meet through the goal? Are you acting 'literally' out of fear or out of love?

Remember, your goal is here to support you. It should improve your present reality. It should motivate you and make you feel good now, not just when you achieve it. If you aren't enjoying the process of achieving your goal but think it's attainment will bring you joy, you're deluding yourself. Joy isn't something you should wait for; it's something you should experience every day. **Your goal should bring you joy right now.**

Also remember, if you have deep issues, like a pervasive sense of being unworthy, achieving more won't usually solve the issue. In reality, the desire to achieve more is often a symptom of intense feelings of worthlessness. Deep issues must be solved by looking inward rather than outward!

Wayne Dyer beautifully wrote, "I am a human being, not a human doing. Don't equate your self-worth with how well you do things in life. You aren't what you do. If you are what you do, then when you don't ... you aren't."

Key Lessons:

Setting realistic goals is important. You don't want to be discouraged because you set a goal that is totally out of reach. To avoid this, make sure you follow this advice:

- Gauge your emotions and see how you feel about your goal. Does it excite you? Do you believe you can achieve it?
- Chunk down your goal into small, manageable tasks you can work on each day or week.

For challenging goals:

- Condition your mind for success by designing a more empowering environment, (refer to "Creating the Right Mindset" for more information).
- Make sure the route to your ambitious goal is enjoyable right now and not just in a hypothetical future.

4. Having A Clear Deadline for Your Goal (T)

 A goal is a dream with a deadline.

— NAPOLEON HILL, AUTHOR OF THINK AND GROW RICH.

Parkinson's Law states "works expand so as to fill the time available for its completion." Without a clear deadline, your productivity may suffer and your ability to achieve your goals may be severely jeopardized.

It is therefore important to give your goals clear deadlines. For instance, it's better to say you'll finish a task by December 31 at 5pm than it is to say you'll finish by the end of the month. With a measurable timeframe for your goals, your chances of success become much higher. I'm sure you'll agree, the previous example of studying Japanese illustrates this very well.

Make certain you set a clear deadline for your goal and commit to it. Break your goal into smaller tasks and set sub-deadlines. This way, you'll know whether you're on track for success. You'll also be able to adjust your efforts and revise your schedule whenever necessary.

Then, take your deadline seriously. Do your best to meet your sub-deadlines one after the other. This will help you build momentum, increase your self-esteem, and strengthen your belief in your ability to achieve your goal. Keep your deadline in mind as you progress towards your goal.

That said, don't beat yourself up if you fail to meet your deadline. Don't overreact and make a huge deal out of it. You don't want to sabotage your efforts and give up on a goal that's meaningful to you just because you failed to meet a specific deadline. As long as you accomplish what you intended, failing to meet an arbitrary deadline isn't a major issue.

Remember, setting realistic goals with realistic deadlines takes time and requires experience, not to mention all the things that may go wrong along the way. In the next section, "Emotionally sustainable", we'll delve deeper into the pitfalls you must avoid when setting goals.

Nobody can be 100% consistent. Things will happen along the way that slow down your progress. That's why you want to remain flexible. For example, I initially intended for this to be a short book written within a correspondingly short amount of time. However, while working on it, I realized it would be better to create something more detailed. I wanted to provide readers with a more comprehensive method, and I knew this meant extending my deadline. (For more on flexibility refer to the section "Other Key Considerations.")

Finally, we must mention there's not much pressure to respect deadlines when it comes to personal development. It's not like work or school where you're constantly held accountable by others. If this lack of pressure is a problem for you, you may need to set up an accountability system. For more on accountability, refer to the last section "Other Key Considerations."

Key Lessons:

Having deadlines for your goals is important. A clear deadline will:

- Make your goal more concrete and increase your chances of reaching it
- Force you to focus on your goal and prevent you from overworking yourself, and
- Require an accountability system, or a high level of self-discipline to be effective—see "Accountability Partner & Mastermind Group" in the section "Other Key Considerations."

* * *

Action step

Write down your deadline using the workbook (*Section III. 4. Having a clear deadline for your goals*).

* * *

5. Having an Emotionally Sustainable Goal (E)

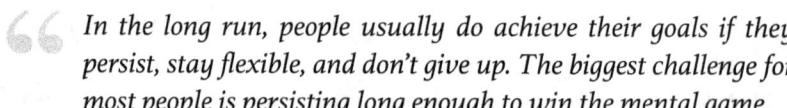
In the long run, people usually do achieve their goals if they persist, stay flexible, and don't give up. The biggest challenge for most people is persisting long enough to win the mental game.

— STEVE PAVLINA, PERSONAL DEVELOPMENT BLOGGER.

Many people give up on their goals as soon as they encounter their first massive setback. I believe this is mostly due to a lack of mental readiness, and I'm convinced it can be avoided with enough mental preparation.

In this section, we're going to cover the psychological aspects of goal setting. More specifically, we'll cover the importance of identifying obstacles and planning for the worst. We'll also discuss how you can reframe failure and overcome self-criticism to achieve your goal.

Identify obstacles

Many people fail to accomplish their goals because they don't take time to identify the obstacles they might encounter or create strategies to overcome them.

Encountering obstacles that could stop you from reaching your goal is inevitable. You must be prepared to overcome these challenges if they begin to stand in your way. And they will! Let's say your goal is to lose weight. The list below summarizes some of the obstacles you may encounter.

- Hunger

- Dinner with friends, because it's difficult to eat healthily when everyone else is eating tempting foods that aren't part of your diet.
- Starbucks, because you're used to going there on your way to work.
- Emotional eating, because you tend to eat a lot when stressed.
- Lack of support, because you're the only one dieting in your family.
- Temptation, because your fridge is full of unhealthy foods.
- A weak "why," because you know you should eat healthily but don't feel motivated enough to do so.

In any of these instances, it would be good to consider what triggers you, what encourages you to eat unhealthy food, and what you can do to work around it. You might empty your fridge of unhealthy foods, join a support group, or enlist your friends to help you stay on track when you're going out with them. If you've tried unsuccessfully to eat healthily or lose weight in the past, you should figure out why it didn't work for you and see what you can learn from your earlier mistakes. It's also advisable to figure out your underlying thoughts surrounding food. Perhaps you associate unhealthy foods or excessive eating and drinking with enjoyable activities such as going to the movies, hanging out with friends, or spending time with family. If so, it would be wise to adopt new beliefs that don't inextricably link these things.

Now it's your turn. What major obstacles are you likely to encounter, and how will you overcome them? Take some time now to write them down using the downloadable worksheet.

* * *

Action step

Refer to the workbook and make a list of all the obstacles you may encounter as you work towards your stated goal. (*Section III. 5a. Identifying the obstacles.*)

* * *

Imagining the worst

We tend to be overly optimistic when we set a goal. I strongly recommend you do the following exercise to offset this:

Think of all the obstacles you may encounter during the journey towards your goal. Now, try to imagine what the worst-case scenario would look like. Don't be realistic. Think of the unexpected and imagine what terrible things could happen. Go wild! Then ask yourself what you'd do if these situations were to actually happen.

How would you feel? What would your reaction be? If you go through this exercise and write them down as a memory aid, you'll feel mentally prepared to face any challenge, and any setbacks you experience won't be able to stop you.

When tough times arrive, use this exercise to remind yourself of what you said you'd be willing to go through to achieve your goal. It's an essential step as it gives you peace of mind, focus, and perseverance, which is something people often lack.

* * *

Action step

Refer to the workbook and write down some of the worst-case scenarios (*Section III. 5b. Imagining the worst*).

* * *

Inoculating yourself against failure

How important is your goal? What are you willing to do to accomplish it? What are you willing to give up?

Let me tell you something: no matter how talented you are, you will fail many times. That's the reality. If you really want to reach your goal, you have to accept this truth first.

Most of us are afraid of failure, but that's a big mistake. Failure is actually one of the most important things in life because it's a necessary step towards success. Part of the reason our minds are so powerful is they operate through a process of trial and error to help us reach our goals. Regardless of your goal, you'll probably make small but frequent adjustments without even realizing it.

Failure is just a sign your actions and objectives have become too misaligned, and it's time to do something about it. You should see failure as your brain's way of telling you you're going in the wrong direction. It's just a sign you need to make some major adjustments to realign your actions with your goal. Failure is the biggest learning opportunity you will ever encounter. Successful people embrace it, unsuccessful people don't.

It's impossible to separate success from failure. Failure is succeeding! That is, it's an integral part of the trial and error process we call success, and it's something you have to go through to reach your goal. Being successful means having a healthy relationship with failure. As long as you learn something from setbacks, you can never truly fail. When you fail (and, at times, you surly will), ask yourself the following question: "What can I learn from this to help me move forward? Remember, it doesn't matter if you fail. Failure is normal. What matters is how you react to it. Don't just make peace with failure; learn to use it to your advantage.

Below are some "failure" stories to inspire you:

- Renowned sculptor Auguste Rodin's father referred to him by saying he had an idiot for a son. Described as the "worst pupil" in school, Rodin failed in all three attempts to gain admittance to art school. His uncle called him "uneducable."
- An expert once said of Vince Lombardi that he "...possesses minimal football knowledge" and "lacks motivation."
- Beethoven was awkward in handling violins and preferred playing his own compositions over improving his technique. His teacher labeled him "hopeless" as a composer.
- The parents of famous opera singer Enrico Caruso wanted him to be an engineer. Worse yet, his teacher felt he lacked a voice and sang poorly.

- Walt Disney was fired by a newspaper editor for a "lack of ideas". He also went bankrupt several times before building Disneyland.
- Thomas Edison's teachers said he was too stupid to learn anything.
- War and Peace author Leo Tolstoy flunked out of college. He was described as being, "...both unable and unwilling to learn."
- Alibaba founder Jack Ma failed primary school tests twice and middle school tests three times. He tried to get into college three times but failed in each attempt. He then applied for jobs but was rejected thirty times. When KFC came to his city, they hired twenty-three out of the twenty-four people who applied—Jack Ma wasn't hired. He applied to Harvard but was rejected ten times.

So-called failures aren't really failures until they give up. As Norman Vincent Peale, author of, The Power of Positive Thinking, said, "It's always too soon to quit."

Make sure you give serious thought to what you're willing to go through to achieve your goal. Doing so is key to your success. Ask yourself the following:

- What would make me give up?
- Am I ready to be ridiculed by my family or friends?
- Can I keep moving forward even if no one believes in me?
- What am I ready to give up in order to achieve my goal? Going out? Going on vacations? Hobbies? Parties?

* * *

Action step

Answer the corresponding questions in the workbook. (*Section III. 5c. Inoculating yourself against failure.*)

* * *

Reconnecting with your "why"

Last but not least, ask yourself why. Why is this goal so important to you? When nobody believes in you, when things are not going well, or when the sacrifices are overwhelming, what will make you persevere?

I encourage you to write down your 'whys' and go through them whenever things are tough. The more you focus on the 'why' of a goal, the more you'll be able to persevere.

It may help to refer to the "Identify the Values Behind your Goals" section of the book when figuring out your 'whys.'

My 'why':

- **Why #1: I will earn money doing what I love.** Being told what to do by others doesn't inspire me, but doing what I love allows me to tap into my intrinsic motivation consistently and to accomplish more. It also grants me independence and allows me to avoid crowded offices and other workspaces that don't mesh well with my introverted personality.
- **Why #2: It gives me the freedom to work whenever and wherever I want.** I'm a French person living in Japan who writes books in English. Not surprisingly, I love to travel, have a long list of countries that I'd like to experience. Earning passive income through my blog gives me the flexibility to travel and live in different countries.
- **Why #3: I will keep learning throughout my life.** I am easily bored and usually tire of repeating the same thing over and over. This frees me from being forced to do the same thing at the same company for the next thirty to forty years.
- **Why #4: I will help hundreds of thousands of people.** I can reach a lot of people through the Internet. It's both exciting and fulfilling to help others improve their lives.
- **Why #5: I will be happier.** I want to inspire people to grow, reach their potential, and find happiness. I must do this for myself if I want to help others do the same.

* * *

Action step

Use the workbook to write down the 'why' behind your goal. (*Section III. 5d. Reconnecting with your whys.*)

* * *

Dealing with self-Criticism the right way

I used to be very hard on myself but, more often than not, it wasn't in my best interest. This often caused me to give up on my goals too easily. You might worry you'll become lazy or complacent if you don't push yourself hard enough, but research shows having self-compassion works better than beating yourself up. I couldn't agree more with this. I've learned to be more compassionate towards myself in the past few months, and it has benefited in a number of ways. Self-criticism isn't good for us, it's related to self-sabotage and is usually the result of insufficient self-esteem.

According to recent studies, those who are more self-compassionate tend to perform better and persevere longer. Can you imagine how much more peace of mind and stability you would have if you were able to stop beating yourself up? The thing is, if you're being hard on yourself you're probably being hard on others as well. Don't get me wrong; I'm not saying you're being mean. You're probably very kind and compassionate with the people you know, but perhaps you're constantly misjudging those you don't know so well in the back of your mind. You might look around and think, "Why is this person eating unhealthily?" or, "Why is that person angry all the time?" or even, "Why is that person so mean?"

If this is you, don't feel bad. All you have to do is become aware of how much you judge others. If you find you are indeed judging people, start allowing them to be the way they are even if you don't like it. Tell yourself it's okay if they do this or that. Accept things as they are and assume these people have problems of their own and are doing the best they can. The more compassionate you are towards other, the more you'll be able to accept yourself for who you are: an imperfect human being among other imperfect human beings.

Interestingly, one of the characteristics of people with healthy self-esteem is the ability to judge their competence accurately. They don't beat themselves up for making mistakes or for failing, nor are they overconfident. In various studies, subjects with high self-esteem have been shown to persist much longer at a task than those with low self-esteem. If you want to know more about self-esteem, I highly encourage you to read *The Six Pillars of Self-Esteem* by Nathaniel Branden. I think it's one of the best books on the subject and contains this great quote: "Self-esteem is the reputation we acquire with ourselves."

To help you assess your level of self-esteem, there follows a brief summary of the six practices (or pillars) of self-esteem, as identified by Nathaniel Branden:

1. **Living consciously:** In Nathaniel Branden's words, "to live consciously means to seek to be aware of everything that bears on our actions, purposes, value, and goals—to the best of our ability, whatever that ability may be—and to behave in accordance with that which we see and know."
2. **Self-acceptance:** Is choosing to value yourself, to treat yourself with respect and stand up for your right to exist. Self-acceptance is the basis upon which self-esteem develops.
3. **Self-responsibility:** Is realizing no one is coming to save you and you are responsible for your life. It is accepting you are responsible for your choices and actions. You are responsible for how you use your time, and for your happiness. Because only *you* can change your life.
4. **Self-assertiveness:** Means, honoring my wants, needs, and values and seeking appropriate forms of their expression in reality.
5. **Living purposefully:** Is to use your powers to achieve the goals you have selected. In other words, it's your ability to set and achieve goals in every area of your life.
6. **Personal integrity:** Is behaving in a way that matches your ideals, convictions and belief. It's when you can look at yourself in the mirror and know you're doing the right thing.

So, what reputation do you have with yourself? Do you beat yourself up regularly? How would your friends feel if you treated them the way you treat yourself?

Practice treating yourself the way you would treat an important houseguest. Be compassionate, and don't let negative self-talk discourage you.

***

Action step

Complete the corresponding exercise in the workbook. (*Section III. 5e. Dealing with self-criticism the right way.*)

***

Avoiding planning pitfalls

In the words of Bill Gates, "*Most people overestimate what they can do in one year and underestimate what they can do in ten years.*"

It's true we tend to be overly optimistic when making plans, especially short-term ones. That's why it's so common to see companies and government institutions going well over their budgets and missing deadlines on new projects. The more ambitious your goal is, the more likely you are to face unforeseeable difficulties. We're only human and certainly can't predict everything. You are likely to overestimate what you can do in one to two years, but you're also likely to underestimate what you can accomplish in five or ten. As such, I recommend you double the original timeframe for your goal.

In many cases, growth is not linear, and you might find you aren't moving forward as quickly as you expected in the first few months or even the first year. That's where most people quit, but don't give in to the urge to let go. Don't surrender. Hold on!

To illustrate the importance of patience and perseverance, motivational speaker Les Brown told the following story of the Chinese Bamboo:

> *The Chinese Bamboo tree takes five years to grow, and when they go through a process of growing it, they have to water and fertilize the ground where it is every day, and it doesn't break through the ground until the fifth year, but once it breaks through the ground within 5 weeks it grows ninety feet tall. The question is: does it grow ninety feet in five weeks or five years. The answer is obvious.*

Real estate investor and motivational speaker, Grant Cardone, recalls when he created his first business at twenty-nine years old. He thought he was prepared for challenges ahead, but he greatly underestimated the amount of effort and time needed to achieve his goal.

> *I assumed it would take three or four months to get back to that income level of the job I previously had. Well, it took me almost three years to get my business to provide me with the same amount of income of my previous job. That was twelve times longer than I had expected. And I almost quit three months into my new business venture. Not because of the money, but because of the amount of resistance and disappointment I was experiencing.*

I hope by now you understand the importance of preparing for the worse.

* * *

Action step

Use the workbook to adjust your deadline (*Section III. 5f. Avoiding planning pitfalls.*)

* * *

6. Strategizing Your Goal (S)

I find it fascinating that most people plan their vacations with better care than their lives. Perhaps that is because escape is easier than change.

— Jim Rohn, author and motivational speaker.

Achieving a goal means going from a point A (where you are now), to point B (where you want to be). There are billions of decisions we can make at any moment in our lives. There is always a way to find one of the many paths that will lead to your goal. Your job is to find it, and you need a clear strategy to do this!

In this section, we'll discuss the strategic aspect of goal setting and what you can do to maximize your chances of achieving your exciting goals. In the business world, companies spend a lot of time strategizing to reach their objectives, and this is exactly what you need to do as well.

Understanding the rules of success

Many people want to achieve something without knowing much about it. If you're serious about a goal, however, you should try to learn everything about it. You can start by purchasing a book or two written by experts in the area that interests you. You need to know the rules of the game if you want to win the match and achieve your goal. Figure out exactly what successful people are doing. How did they get there? What is their mindset? What are their daily habits? What challenges did they have to overcome? These are important questions to answer.

First and foremost, knowing this enables you to anticipate many of the difficulties you'll encounter. You'll be able to prepare mentally for those challenges and figure out ways to overcome them.

This knowledge will also help eliminate your limiting beliefs little by little. After all, the more examples you find of people who have accomplished what you wish to achieve, the more attainable your goal will appear.

Also, you'll be able to figure out why those who didn't reach the goal failed. You don't need to reinvent the wheel. **Spend as much time learning from people's failures as you do from their successes, and use the information/knowledge to reduce your learning curve.** You can't afford to overlook anything.

You should always be on the lookout for new information that will either help you to achieve your goal faster, or increase your chances of success. **Thorough planning is essential.**

Example:

How can I cut the learning curve when building my blog?

1. Read books written by people who have created high-traffic websites.
2. Join online communities of people who are creating successful websites.
3. Identify great websites from experts in blog creation.

* * *

Action step

Answer the questions in the corresponding section of the workbook. (*Section III. 6a. Understanding the rule of success.*)

* * *

Filling in the gap

Achieving a goal is always a matter of going from a point A to point B. Ask yourself what skills you must develop in order to reach your goal and figure out how to bridge the gap. **Identify the skills, if worked on daily, will help you the most to achieve your goal.**

Let's use my website as an example:

What skills do I need to build a successful blog?

1. Marketing skills.
2. The effective use of social media.
3. Finding and mastering the most efficient ways to create lasting traffic.
4. The ability to discern what my readers will find interesting and useful.
5. SEO (search engine optimization) skills.
6. Creating engaging, well-written, and inspiring articles.

What about you? What skills do you need to work on to reach your goal?

Questions to Consider:

1. What could possibly prevent me from succeeding?
2. Am I doing everything I need to do to reach my goal?
3. If I keep doing what I'm doing today/this week/this month, am I going to reach my goal?

* * *

Action step

Use the workbook to write down the specific skill(s) you need to develop to achieve your goal. (*Section III. 6a1. Filling the gap.*)

* * *

Using the 80/20 rule

When it comes to the work involved in reaching your goals, some things will have more impact than others. The 80/20 rule states that 20% of your efforts will account for 80% of your results. This ratio is only a rough indicator, but it's helpful nonetheless.

It's essential you identify the things which will have the most impact and focus most of your time on them. Make it a habit to start your morning with them. Review your progress on a regular basis, and don't use less important tasks to trick yourself into thinking you're working when you aren't.

If you doubt the effectiveness of focusing on a few key tasks, consider this excerpt from Gary Keller's book The One Thing. It illustrates the importance of focusing on a few key things rather than trying to do to many things at once.

 As fast as we were growing, we were still not acknowledged by the top people in our industry. I challenged our group to brainstorm one hundred ways to turn this situation around. It took us all day to come up with the list. The next morning, we narrowed the list down to ten ideas, and from there we chose just one big idea. The one that we decided on was that I would write a book on how to become an elite performer in our industry. It worked. Eight years later that one book had not only become a national bestseller, but also had morphed into a series of books with total sales of over a million copies. In an industry of about a million people, one thing changed our image forever.

Finding your top 20% tasks

The first step to identifying the 20% of your tasks that generate 80% of your results is making a list of all the things you could do to achieve your goal. Try to come up with at least 20 different things. If you've already started to work on your goals, write down all the things you're doing in relation to them. Then come up with as many new ideas as possible.

The second step involves asking yourself the following question: If I could only do one thing on this list, which one would help me make the most progress toward my goal? Draw a circle around this task. Repeat the process until you come up with a list of three to five tasks. That's the top 20% tasks you need to focus on most.

Eliminating distractions

While some tasks produce tangible results, others are distractions in disguise. They include things like watching videos on YouTube, or reading books passively. For more awareness of these tasks, try writing them down. Consider them your 'not-to-do' list.

* * *

Action step

Use the workbook to write down your most important tasks and create your 'not-to-do list'. (*Section III. 6a2 Using the 80/20 rule.*)

* * *

Learning new skills with deliberate practice

For the most part, you can learn any skills you need to achieve your goals. These days, we live in a world where we're often one click away from the knowledge we need. Once you've identified the skills you need and the tasks you should focus on, it's time to master and complete them.

When you work on developing new skills, the way you practice is more important than the amount of time you spend practicing (quality beats quantity). Let's take someone who plays tennis for thirty years as an example. You'd think that playing for thirty years would make them a pro. If they've only played casually with friends, however, it's likely their skill level isn't much better than it was when they started. Research shows hard work and deliberate practice are more important than talent when it comes to achieving goals. **"I'm not talented enough" isn't a valid excuse.**

Deliberate practice involves meticulous training that focuses on the things/skills necessary to improve your performance. More often than not, it's mentally taxing, involves a lot a repetitive work, requires constant feedback, and isn't much fun. It's no surprise few people are willing to commit to it as intensely as those at the top of their fields do.

Sadly, this is why so many of us are stuck. Sure, we can enjoy playing a certain instrument, or we have fun playing a particular sport with our friends. This doesn't mean we're willing to practice the same thing thousands of times, run every morning, work out consistently, or anything else that's tough, demanding, and requires unswerving commitment. The reality is we're unwilling to put in the work required to go the next level. This is what keeps us stuck, not a lack of talent.

For a great example of intense, deliberate practice, let's take a look at Benjamin Franklin and how he became a great writer. Franklin took laborious steps to improve his writing style, vocabulary, and organizational skills. He mastered the first skill by making notes on articles from *Spectator*, a high-quality newspaper, which he would use to rewrite the articles a few days later. He would then compare his version to the original and modify it accordingly. He mastered the second skill by rewriting *Spectator* essays in verse and then in prose so he could compare his vocabulary to the vocabulary used in the original article. He mastered organization by writing summaries of every sentence in a particular article on separate sheets of paper. He would then wait a few weeks before challenging himself to write the article in the correct order and comparing his work to the original article.

Those three exercises required a lot of mental effort, focused on specific skills, involved long periods of repetition, and certainly weren't fun. What's impressive is Franklin practiced these exercises consistently while working full time in his brother's printing business. His methods would probably be effective today, but how many people would be willing to go through this kind of tedious, deliberate practice on a consistent basis? Very few.

The bottom line is this: **There's no skill you can't develop if you're firmly committed to your goal** and have the basic mental and physical capacities required. Some skills might be easy to develop while others may require hard work and deliberate practice; it all depends on the difficulty of your goal and what your starting point is.

* * *

Action step

Write down what you'll do to master the skills required to achieve your goal (*Section III. 6a4. Learning new skills with deliberate practice*).

* * *

Leveraging the power of daily habits

Speaking of the philosophy of Aristotle, historian William Durant, wrote: *"We are what we repeatedly do. Excellence, then, is not an act, but a habit."*

What you do on a daily basis is what will ultimately determine whether or not you'll be successful. Reaching your long-term goals depends on your daily habits. However, it's hard to think long-term in a fast-paced world whose products and advertisements encourage instant gratification. The fact remains, in the long run, adopting certain habits brings many benefits. Meditating for a few minutes a day, taking the time to express gratitude, or scheduling the upcoming day, for example, can create positive changes that significantly impact your life.

If running a marathon is your big goal, preparing a week before the event probably won't cut it. If exercise isn't something you're used to, you'll have to start small and gradually increase the intensity and duration of your training until you can handle the physical activity required to reach your goal.

Building momentum through daily action

There's nothing better than daily actions to build momentum. When you work on your goal every day, you'll build momentum that will stay with you as long as you remain consistent.

For instance, if you want to start a business, you could begin by checking out books on business creation. The next day, you could decide which books to buy. The day after that, you could seek the advice of someone you know who owns a business. By taking a succession of daily baby steps, you make the goal part of your reality. In doing so, your belief in your ability to succeed will increase. This will allow you to create a new, empowering belief system that will slowly but surely replace your old one.

Turning tasks into daily habits

Almost any task can become a daily habit. Breaking your goals down into daily habits helps build momentum and automate the achievement process. Unsurprisingly, this will vastly increase your chances of success.

If your goal is to write a book, you could write one page every day first thing in the morning. If you want to learn a language, your goal could be to study it for thirty minutes daily.

Starting small

To avoid attaching negative feelings to your new task, start small and do what feels comfortable. Choose a time commitment that you can stick with on a daily basis. Then, once it becomes automatic, you can gradually increase the time commitment as needed.

If you want to meditate for an hour a day, you could start with a minute a day if that's what feels manageable. If you want to run several miles a day, you should start with a few minutes each day. Once these practices become habit, you can spend more and more time on them. The amount of time you start with isn't important. **The point is to create a new habit and build momentum.**

Set "if ... then" triggers

Our day is a succession of small actions. Most of them, such as waking, showering, eating breakfast, brushing our teeth, and leaving the house, are automatic. We don't have to think about them to do them. You can take advantage of this by using the end of an action that is already automatic as a trigger for a new habit, which will help make the new habit automatic. "If ... then" triggers are a great way to do this, and can be seen in the following examples:

1. **If** I have just woken up, **then** I'll immediately drink a glass of water.
2. **If** I have just finished showering, **then** I'll immediately meditate.

3. **If** I just came home from work, **then** I'll immediately start working on my goal.

Setting triggers helps you save energy and prevent your willpower from depleting by creating habits that will become automatic after a while. Studies show that setting intentions can prevent willpower burnout.

For a detailed, step-by-step method on how to set long-lasting habits, refer to the second book in this bundle, *Habits That Stick, The Ultimate Guide to Building Powerful Habits that Stick Once and For All.*

* * *

Action step

Use the workbook to write down the three tasks you'll perform every day to reach your goal. (*Section III. 6a4. Leveraging the power of daily habits.*)

* * *

Investing in your goals

You may be wondering whether you should invest in commercial software, books, and courses, or stick to free stuff online. If you have a lot of free time, the second option might work. You can find some amazing resources that way. However, they might be disorganized and finding the information you want is usually time-consuming.

Consider the following: If you search for the best possible way to learn the skill you need, you're going to find resources that throngs of people have purchased and used with success. Such programs must be worth as much if not more than their cost. Otherwise, no one would buy them.

Furthermore, time is money. Something that costs $100 might sound expensive until you ask yourself how much time you can save by purchasing it. You should also ask yourself how much you value an hour of your time. If the book or program allows you to save 10 hours of your time, for instance, you could invest this time in a part-time job. Let's assume you can find a part-time job that pays $10 an hour. If so, you'll earn $100, the cost of the program! Now, it doesn't seem that expensive.

Of course, the benefits of a particular program also extend to the value they create. If it's a popular product that helps a lot of people, it creates value. Value comes in many forms. You might make more money in the long run by using the program, but your gains might also be emotional. Perhaps it creates a sense of well-being or more satisfaction in life. It's up to you to decide upon a monetary value for non-monetary benefits.

Having an effective method you can follow step by step will also allow you to stay focused on your goal and avoid distractions. You don't want to spend all your time trying to figure out what does and doesn't work. It's best to find something you can trust from start to finish.

Last but not least, investing money gives you more incentive to take action. It shows your commitment to your goals. You're more likely to take action toward your goal if you hire a coach for $500 per month than if you found one offering pro bono services. Similarly, you'd be less likely to take action if you'd downloaded this e-book for free. Free isn't always in your best interest.

Remember, taking action is always the most important thing. As long as you put the advice of the coach, book, or product to use, your investment will be a good one.

Questions to consider:

1. How reliable is the program that I want to use?
2. How much time can I save by purchasing it, and how much do I value an hour of my time?
3. How much money will it allow me to make or save in the long run?
4. To what extent will it allow me to avoid distractions?
5. Does it provide other benefits (such as peace of mind or incentive to take action)?

If, after answering these questions, you feel that the cost is less than the time or money it will save, make the investment.

If you're short on cash and lack the education necessary to earn more money, it's crucial to invest in your education, even if it means substantial sacrifices. Otherwise, you'll be stuck where you are. There are boundless resources in today's world, and many of them are available at a very low cost. We lack neither resourcefulness nor options. Finding, investing in, and making full use of these resources is one of the keys to success.

Key Lessons:

To reach your goals, you must implement the right strategy in the following ways:

- **Understanding the rules of success:** Learn as much as you can from the successes and failures of people who have achieved what you want.
- **Filling in the gap:** Identify all the skills you must develop to go from where you are to where you want to be.
- **Leveraging the 80/20 Principle:** Prioritize like a champion. Focus on the 20% of tasks that produce 80% of your results. Get rid of the rest as much as you can.
- **Using deliberate practice:** You can learn any skill you need. Focus on your core skills and become so good at them that people take notice!
- **Forming daily habits:** Organize your daily tasks around your core skills and high-value tasks. Remain consistent and stick to your habits **each day**. Finally, automate your tasks by setting 'if … then' triggers.
- **Investing in your goals:** Knowledge is the best investment you'll ever make. Make sure you invest your money in books and programs that can accelerate your success.

Scheduling for success

The things that get scheduled are the things that get done.

— ROBIN SHARMA, AUTHOR AND LEADERSHIP SPEAKER.

The more specific your plans are, the more likely you are to achieve your goal. Make a habit of planning your month at the start of each month, planning your week every Sunday morning, and planning your day before you go to bed. I always accomplish a lot more when I plan than when I don't. According to Brian Tracy, a leading expert in goal setting and time management, each minute you spend in planning saves as much as 10 minutes in execution. Make sure you don't skip this important component of the goal setting process!

Planning your month like a pro

A month is a big enough chunk of time for you to make concrete progress towards your goal. When you set monthly goals, you want to focus on a few tasks or projects you'd like to complete by the end of the month. I recommend focusing on three to six projects or tasks related to your goal. Ask yourself this: What tasks, if completed by the end of the month, will allow me to make the most progress toward my goal?

To create your monthly goals, set aside a few hours at the beginning of the month or the end of the previous month. Then do the following:

- Reflect on the progress you made during the month. Look at your previous goals and see whether you've achieved them or not. Here are two questions to ask yourself:
- What went well? What do I want to congratulate myself on?
- What could I have done better?
- What will I stop/start doing this month to improve my results?
- Review your long-term goals (e.g. the yearly ones) and your overall strategy to achieve them. Adjust your long-term goals if necessary.
- Write down the three to five projects or tasks you want to work on this month. These should be tasks that will allow you to make significant progress on your goal. Again, make sure your tasks follow the **SMARTEST Goal Method** and can be easily measured.

Create the habit of setting and reviewing goals every month. It will allow you to make great progress.

Final tip: Set a specific day and time each month that you stick to. Show up as you would for any formal meeting.

Planning your week like a pro

Identify three goals you want to accomplish during the week to get closer to your goal. These should be the best things you can do to move forward. To give a personal example, my goals could be as follows:

1. Completing a specific chapter of this book.
2. Writing one article and submitting it to major personal development websites.
3. Creating free content for my readers, which, at the moment, involves working on a chapter of another e-book.

I tend to be all over the place, so it helps to have a reminder of these goals whenever I need it. It keeps me from getting lost in irrelevant details and wasting time on things that don't help me accomplish anything.

Note that your three goals may not be the same every week—it all depends on the specifics regarding your particular goal. In my case, my main tasks would involve writing, but they could also involve promotion or marketing.

Make sure you set aside specific times to schedule the upcoming week. This way, you'll reach optimal results.

Planning your day like a pro

Before we have a detailed discussion on how to plan your day for maximum effectiveness, let me give you seven reasons why you should plan your day.

1. **To avoid distraction:** When you know exactly what you need to do, you prevent your brain coming up with reasons to procrastinate. Whenever you put yourself in a situation where you have to think about what to do next, you give your brain an

opportunity to look for distractions. You might feel the sudden urge to check your emails, go on Facebook, or watch videos on YouTube. If you're not careful, you can easily waste hours on these things. Be aware your mind will almost always try to distract you, and be on the lookout for the ways in which this shows.

2. **To reflect on your strategy**: Planning gives you an opportunity to step back and look at the bigger picture. You can assess the efficiency of what you're doing and make sure you're focusing your energy on the things that are truly important.
3. **To limit the use of willpower**: Your willpower is a limited resource. Advance planning gives your subconscious a sense of direction. When this happens, you don't have to think much about what you need to do next. Your behavior becomes automated, and you don't need willpower to motivate yourself before each and every task.
4. **To build momentum**: Once you complete your first task in the morning, you feel a sense of accomplishment and relief, and this builds momentum for the rest of the day. This sense of momentum compels you to accomplish more throughout the day and helps create an effortless source of motivation.
5. **To increase self-esteem**: Many people fail to realize that self-esteem is linked to discipline. The more you discipline yourself to do what's needed, the better your self-esteem will be.
6. **To boost your productivity**: Completing your most important task first and focusing on one thing at a time will greatly increase your productivity.
7. **To reduce stress**: Planning ahead and knowing exactly what you'll have to do each day will bring you peace of mind. It will also decrease the amount of uncertainty you'll experience throughout your day. All you need is to complete the items on your to-do list one by one. It doesn't require much thinking and you won't be overwhelmed by all the things you need to do.

Now, let's see how you can plan your day to ensure it's a productive one.

Before going to bed make a list of three to five tasks that will help you move toward your goal. Now look at the list and ask yourself, "If I could accomplish only one task on this list, which one would have the most impact?"

Make a commitment to complete whichever task you choose first thing in the morning, and repeat the same process for the rest of the items on your day's list. Don't check your emails, read the newspaper, or watch television. Avoid anything that could distract you until you've finished at least two of the most important tasks.

Finally, whenever possible, set a specific time to plan your daily activities. **The more you plan the more efficient you'll be.**

Additional tip:

To further increase your productivity, you can visualize your day. Here is how to do it:

- After you plan your day, take at least five minutes to visualize it. See yourself accomplishing everything on your list. Picture your day going exactly as you want it to. Your subconscious mind will work with those images of success while you sleep.
- Repeat the process the next morning before you start your day. Setting your intention is an important part of staying on track and has been proven to increase willpower

Creating your list of goals

I highly recommend creating a yearly list of goals. It helps to divide your list into categories. When you categorize your goals, you decrease the chances of neglecting some parts of your life in favor of others. Better still, breaking long-term goals into annual ones makes them much easier to achieve. You can then break your goals down into monthly and weekly ones as discussed earlier.

The steps below can make creating your list easier and more efficient:

1. Use positive words and statements that show confidence in your ability to accomplish those goals. Use phrases such as 'I am,' 'I will easily,' or 'I will definitely,' when describing your intention.
2. Look over your list every morning.

3. Adjust your aims over time. You probably won't accomplish all your goals, and this is okay. Get rid of the goals that no longer resonate with you or can be postponed. Focus instead on the most important goals, the ones that will provide the greatest contribution to your fulfillment.

Remember: Don't stress out trying to achieve ever single goal you set. You won't achieve every single one, and this is perfectly normal!

You may have many different things you wish to achieve. However, it's important to focus on the ones that matter most and avoid trying to accomplish all of them at once. You will inevitably drop some goals over time, but you should always start by spending the majority of your time on the goals that excite you the most.

As previously mentioned, it's useful to apply the 80/20 rule for your goals. Focus on your most important goals. Focus is key! Ask yourself which goal you would choose if you could only accomplish one on the list. To prioritize your goals, repeat the process until you've gone through the entire list.

Key Lessons:

The better you plan, the more likely you are to achieve your goals. As stated earlier, failing to prepare is preparing to fail. So, make sure you do the following four things:

1. **Plan your month like a pro:** At the beginning of each month, set aside some time to write down your monthly goals. Identify three to five core tasks you'd like to work on.
2. **Plan your week like a pro:** At the beginning of each week, identify three core tasks that will move you closer to your goals. Make sure you schedule them.
3. **Plan your day like a pro:** Write down three to five tasks you want to work on. It's best to do this in the morning or before bed the previous night. Then, rank all the tasks in order of importance and work on the most important one first. Go down the list until you complete all of your tasks.

4. **Create your list of yearly goals:** Write down your yearly goals and look at them often. Make sure you have goals in every important area of your life.

7. Transferring Your Goal to the Subconscious (T)

 The war has begun and it's between you and you. There ain't nobody else in your way.

— Anonymous.

When your subconscious mind lines up with your goals, you can achieve exceptional things. When it works against you, however, it often seems as though you're driving with the brakes on. When that's the case, you need more than a great strategy to achieve your goal.

In this section, we'll discuss how you can befriend your subconscious mind and overcome limiting beliefs. Then we'll see how you can reprogram your mind for success through daily conditioning. This will allow you to develop the necessary mindset to achieve your goals.

What are 'limiting beliefs'?

Limiting beliefs are the assumptions upon which we base our lives, which is why it's so important to know which ones are holding us back. Our reality is the result of our beliefs, and our worlds are limited by what we think is possible. These thoughts do not necessarily reflect the truth. What we believe we can do may be entirely different from what we can do in actuality. The first step to letting go of our limiting beliefs is to accept they are the subjective truth rather objective—they are not necessarily the actual truth.

Limiting beliefs can hold you back and create a reality that isn't the one you want. Your subconscious mind will always act in concert with your thoughts, even if you aren't aware of them. Beliefs are simply thoughts repeated so often and for so long your subconscious mind has accepted them as true. They are the reflection of your personal interpretation of the things your parents, friends, or the media have repeatedly told you. As such, the beliefs you hold may not be yours. It's entirely possible you've inherited them from your parents, who possibly inherited them from their own parents. Or, they might be the result of negative experiences in your past. Fortunately, there's no rule that says you must stick with a particular belief, especially the ones you haven't consciously chosen. It's vital to understand you are not your mind, your thoughts, or your limiting beliefs. You are, in fact, the observer of your mind and the perceiver of your thoughts, and you can choose which thoughts to entertain and which thoughts to ignore.

A four-step process to overcome limiting beliefs

Step 1 - Identifying your limiting beliefs

In which areas of your life are you unhappy? Where are you being held back? Do you already have any negative beliefs?

Look at each area of your life one by one and ask yourself, "What are the real reasons I'm unsatisfied in this area?" If you consider the thoughts arise in response to this question, you'll be able to figure out what you're thinking and what stories you're telling yourself.

One thing I recommend you to do is to look at a wheel of life and figure out the area in which your biggest goal belongs—to find it online, simply google "wheel of life." How well is this area of your life going? Do you honestly believe you can achieve your goal? If not, what limiting beliefs are telling you you can't?

Some areas to consider:

- Career
- Family
- Finance
- Health
- Personal Growth
- Relationships
- Social Life

Now it's time to develop a better understanding of just how a limiting belief can affect you. Let's use, 'I'm not good enough,' a very common limiting belief, as our example. This belief causes the following side effects:

- **Procrastination.** You'll want to put things off and think along the lines of, "I'll do it later. I don't feel confident, and I would fail if I do it now."
- **Quitting.** You'll find yourself looking for reasons to give up and you'll want to quit at the smallest sign of failure, be it real or imagined. You'll say, "See! I told you I'm not good enough."
- **Self-sabotage.** To ensure your failure and validate your feelings of incompetence and worthlessness, you will set goals that are too big to be accomplished in too short a timeframe.

Realizing the constant warfare between you and your subconscious is half the battle. Having negative thoughts is normal, but you should *never* allow them to prevent you from moving forward. It's okay to acknowledge your negative thoughts, but you shouldn't accept them as if they were the ultimate truth.

Your mind might tell you repeatedly you aren't good enough, or you can't do this or that, but your thoughts and feelings are not who you are. You are the individual who observes these feelings. People often use "I am" statements when discussing their emotions, such as "I'm sad" or "I'm angry," but these words are misleading. We ourselves aren't sad or angry, we just *feel* sad or angry. It isn't our identity. Think of feelings as mental clouds passing through your mind. They'll disappear as soon as you accept them and let them go.

When you have negative thoughts, welcome them. Focus on your body and feel the way they manifest within you. Then, give yourself permission to let them go. Accepting you have an unwanted thought doesn't mean accepting it as true. It only means you welcome the thought, realize it doesn't define you, and make a conscious choice to discard it.

Step 2 - Befriending your subconscious mind

The second step is to identify the intention behind the limiting belief. Your subconscious mind is always trying to protect you. It does whatever it can to help you. However, it doesn't necessarily know what can truly help you. Don't fight it, instead, befriend it and collaborate with it. Can you identify the positive intention behind your limiting belief? How is your subconscious mind trying to help you?

Step 3 - Arguing with your subconscious mind

After befriending your subconscious mind, the third step involves arguing with it.

Ask yourself the following question: Is this limiting belief true all the time in every possible situation? Then, look for evidence showing you it isn't. To continue with our previous example, look for all possible evidence that you *are* good enough and you *can* achieve your goal. For instance, you can look at past successes.

Start arguing with your mind on a daily basis. When your mind says you aren't good enough, ask yourself what you *are* good enough to do. Asking this question on a daily basis allows you gradually to deconstruct the belief. If you keep focusing on what you're good enough to do, it will eventually become habitual and you'll begin seeing more and more things you do well.

Start small. The idea is to train your mind to focus on what makes you good enough. When you do this, your subconscious mind will learn to scan your environment for supporting evidence. Remember, if you focus on a thought long enough it will ultimately become a belief.

Examples:

- I'm good enough at cleaning my desk
- I'm good enough to make friends
- I'm good enough to learn a foreign language
- I'm good enough to study
- I'm good enough to exercise.

You can probably come up with thousands of reasons why you *are* good enough.

Gather written evidence

Start writing all your accomplishments in a journal. Or better yet, start writing every single thing you accomplish on a piece of paper and put each one in a jar. Then watch the jar fill up as the weeks pass. You'll notice there are countless things you can do well. There are also things you aren't so good at, but we all have challenges to overcome. Nobody's perfect. Does this mean you're not good enough? I would seriously challenge this assumption.

If you use the above method, eventually, you'll realize unworthiness is not part of your identity. You'll also realize it applies in very limited situations in your life, if any. It will soon become clear to you that you *are* good enough.

You don't have to stop there, however, you can repeat this process for each of your limiting beliefs. If "I'm too old to *insert your goal here*" is your limiting belief, you can gather examples of people who achieved amazing things in their seventies, eighties, nineties, or even hundreds. Fauna Singh ran a marathon at over 100-years-old! You can write your successes in a notebook and even add pictures.

Keep gathering evidence, and soon enough, you'll realize your belief is just that: a belief and not fact.

Step 4 - Replacing your limiting belief with a more empowering one

To create your new, empowering belief, all you have to do is look to its opposite. In the case of 'I'm not good enough,' you could replace it with 'I'm worthy.' You could further specify it to address your needs.

- I'm worthy of love.
- I'm worthy of success.
- I'm worthy of having an amazing girlfriend/boyfriend.
- I'm worthy of achieving *insert your goal here*.

Bonus step

Write a letter to your subconscious mind that you can read out loud whenever you're faced with limiting thoughts or feel like giving up. Your subconscious mind is always trying to help you, but it often does so in ways that are, in actuality, totally unhelpful. When you realize your subconscious has good intentions and begin working with it, however, it'll be much easier to deal with your limiting beliefs. Below is an example of the kind of letter you might want to write for this step:

Dear Subconscious Mind,

You're telling me I'm not good enough. I know your intentions are good and this is your way of protecting me. I'm very grateful, but you don't need to do it anymore. I want to let you know I actually am good enough. I fully deserve to achieve my goal, and I'm completely worthy of it. I can handle failures because they're getting me closer to my goal. I'm learning a lot from them and am actually excited about failing more in the future. After all, each failure brings me one step closer to reaching my goal. I'm asking you to trust supporting me in my journey towards the goal that means so much to me. Thanks for your support!

Key Lessons:

Many people fail to achieve their goals because of the mental blocks and limiting beliefs they hold. Follow these steps to overcome them:

1. Be aware of the ways in which your mind is trying to make you give up. Accept your unwanted thoughts, realize you are not these thoughts. Allow yourself to let go of them.
2. Befriend your subconscious mind and identify the positive intentions behind your limiting beliefs
3. Challenge your limiting beliefs on a daily basis by looking for evidence of their falseness. Be on the lookout for new examples of limiting beliefs and gather written evidence.
4. Replace your old beliefs with new, empowering ones and create a affirmations from them.

BONUS step: Write a letter to your subconscious mind and read it aloud regularly.

* * *

Action step

Go through the four-step process using the workbook (*Section III. 7a. Four-step process to overcome limiting beliefs*).

* * *

Creating the right mindset

> *Successful people are not supermen. Success does not require a super-intellect. Nor is there anything mystical about success. And success isn't based on luck. Successful people are just ordinary folks who have developed belief in themselves and what they do.*
>
> — DAVID J. SCHWARTZ, THE MAGIC OF THINKING BIG.

Choosing thoughts that serve you well

I'm always surprised to see how many people complain incessantly and insist everything is wrong in the world. They're always saying the economy is bad, all the politicians are corrupt, and everything is unfair. Some people are always complaining about the things they have no control over. Yet, there is no rule saying we have to focus on negative things all the time, or worry over that which we can't change. **Overcoming worrying requires action, and you can't do anything useful if you have no control over a particular situation.** If you can't or aren't able to do anything about a situation, you shouldn't waste time thinking about it. Ever.

Who says you need to allow negative thoughts to dwell in your mind? The quality of your thoughts will determine the quality of your life and

you are responsible for what you allow into your mind. Unfortunately, negative thoughts and criticisms have a stronger impact than positive thoughts and praise, which is why it's so important to spend more time focusing on our positive thoughts. Taking the time to fill your mind with positive thoughts will ultimately cause your mind to generate more of them.

Our thoughts are not reality; they are merely our *interpretation* of reality. Our interpretation can be positive or negative. If you don't like your current interpretation of reality, change it by focusing on what you want, and you should do this as often as possible.

If you set ambitious goals during the exercises in this book—and I hope you did—someone around you will probably tell you one or more of your goals are unrealistic. But, have you ever thought about what the phrase, 'It is not realistic' means? It really has no meaning because it's completely subjective. When someone refers to your goals as 'unrealistic,' they're really saying: "What you're trying to accomplish isn't in line with my reality. My current belief system doesn't allow me to see it as possible." Of course, their reality is *not* your reality. Obviously, if you set big goals without doing what it takes to accomplish them, nothing will happen. But it's a totally different story if you choose the right goals, break them down, plan carefully, maintain the right mindset, and consistently take action. Doing these things will help you realize that your goal *is* possible, no matter what it is. I'm not saying it will be easy or you're guaranteed to accomplish it, but it's definitely possible!

Turning into a full-blown optimist

The difference between an optimist and a pessimist is what they choose to focus on. The pessimist chooses to see the glass as half empty while the optimist chooses to see it as half full—even though the volume of water in the glass is the same! Some people may argue optimists are out of touch with reality, but that would be a gross misinterpretation of optimism. Being optimistic doesn't mean denying reality. It just means making a conscious choice to focus on the positive side of things. It also means acknowledging unpleasant aspects of reality but choosing not to dwell on them. There is no law forcing us to concentrate on things that make us miserable. Remember, our unconscious mind is constantly eavesdropping on our thoughts, and those thoughts create our reality.

Unfortunately, most people spend the bulk of their time worrying about useless things. This was illustrated well by Earl Nightingale, a famous motivational speaker who said the following:

> *Let me show you how much time we waste in worrying about the wrong problems. Here is a reliable estimate of things people worry about: Things that never happen 40%, things that are over and past and that can never be changed by all the worry in the world 30%, needless worries about our health 12%, petty miscellaneous worries 10%, really, legitimate worries 8%. In short, **92% of the average person's worries take up valuable time, cause painful stress even mental anguish, and are absolutely unnecessary.***

Are you worrying about useless things?

If you're prone to worry and have a difficult time being optimistic, these tips will help you become a genuinely optimistic person:

1. Stop watching so much TV.
2. Stop reading and watching the news or, at the very least, do so weekly instead of daily.
3. Never buy into other people's 'reality' or pessimism.
4. Stop hanging out with negative people. If that's not an option, seek to limit your time with them as much as possible.
5. Read, watch, or listen to motivational books or videos on a daily basis. I recommend Chicken Soup for the Soul by Jack Canfield, which contains many short but inspiring stories. You might also want to take a look at motivational videos on YouTube.
6. Train yourself to reframe all situations into opportunities or learning experiences, no matter how bad they are. This may sound difficult, but I assure you it's possible! You can find something positive about any situation. It could be something as simple as making you stronger, or being proud of yourself, for working hard to maintain a great attitude in spite of your

difficulties. What happens to you doesn't matter, but how you choose to react to it does.

Visualizing your way to success

> *Your nervous system cannot tell the difference between an imagined experience and a 'real' experience. In either case, it reacts automatically to information which you give to if from your forebrain. Your nervous system reacts appropriately to what 'you' think or imagine to be true.*
>
> — MAXWELL MATLZ, PSYCHO-CYBERNETICS.

When it comes to developing ourselves and improving our lives, imagination is one of the most powerful tools available. Our imagination allows us to create whatever experiences we want at any given time. You can enjoy various scenarios and situations in your mind as often as you want and at no monetary cost. In fact, professional athletes, chess players, army generals, CEOs, and other successful people use visualization on a daily basis. We all use visualization, even if unconsciously. However, if you're like most people, you're probably visualizing negative things. You might be worrying about the future and visualizing yourself losing your job or failing an exam. You might also be dwelling on past failures.

In reality, we can't clearly distinguish real experiences from "fake" ones, which means we can trick our minds by simulating desired experiences through visualization. The more details you visualize, the more your brain will interpret the experience as real. If you feel you lack imagination, don't worry, imagination is like a muscle, and visualization is a great opportunity to strengthen it.

In the 1960s, an experiment was conducted to evaluate students on their ability to make free throws in basketball under various conditions. Students were divided into three groups. The first group was asked to train twenty minutes a day for twenty days, a second was asked not to train at all, and the third was asked to imagine themselves making free throws twenty minutes a day for twenty days. Ultimately, the group of students who practiced only in their imagination performed almost as well as those who practiced in reality. Specifically, those who practiced improved their scores by 24% while those who practiced in their imaginations improved by 23%. Students who refrained from both visualization and physical training showed no improvement. This experiment has been replicated many times since and has continued to produce similar results.

More surprisingly, studies have shown it is possible to build strength and fuel weight loss just by using visualization techniques! One experiment sought to measure the increases in strength among three different groups of people. Those in the group who used audio CDs to visualize working out, improved their strength at a rate similar to those who actually worked out. At the end of the two-week experiment, the group that engaged in 'virtual' workouts improved their strength by 24%, while the group that carried out actual physical exercised improved by 28%!

Visualization is an effective way to influence your subconscious mind and mold it little by little. The more you visualize your goal, the more confident you'll feel about your ability to achieve it. Visualization will give you the motivation and the drive necessary to continue moving forward. It will also encourage your subconscious mind to focus on what you want rather than what you don't want. This will ultimately help you overcome your limiting beliefs and avoid self-sabotage.

As you continue to align yourself with your goal, you'll find yourself doing and trying things you wouldn't have dared to previously. For me, visualizing my goals has helped me take more action towards achieving them. It has also caused me to redefine continually what's possible for me.

Focusing on what you want is vital, so take a few minutes every morning to visualize your goals.

When you visualize, it's key to put yourself in a positive emotional state. Imagine how you'd feel if you had already accomplished your goal. Practice this on a daily basis. The more you can remain in such an empowering emotional state, the more resourceful you'll become. You'll feel more inspired, more creative, and more confident, which will cause you to take more action towards your goal.

Creating a vision board to supercharge your dream

 We have to see ourselves there long before it happens.

— Eric Thomas, motivational speaker.

You might want to create a vision board. A vision board, or dream board as it's sometimes called, is a board where you gather all your goals. Use pictures to symbolize your goals, and allow you to visualize them all simultaneously. You could use a picture of a nice home to signify your dream house, a book to signify the novel you want to publish, or a happy couple to signify your ideal relationship. The possibilities are endless. Put your vision board in a place where you can see it every day. Keep in mind you can create a digital vision board to use as a wallpaper or screensaver on your computer.

Despite what movies like *The Secret* might tell you, a vision board alone won't allow you to magically achieve your goals. It will, however, help you focus on your goals and make them more concrete within your mind. This will ultimately influence your subconscious. The mind is very good at finding information pertinent to the things you tell it to focus on, but don't forget to couple your focus with action!

You might believe many things are out of your reach, but have you ever asked yourself *why* you hold this belief? Are they truly out of reach from an objective standpoint, or does your current, subjective reality make them seem this way?

When you start building a more positive mindset, work on overcoming your limiting beliefs, and visualize your goals as often as possible, you'll gradually create a new reality. As you close the gaps between your thoughts and your goals, you'll be doing more and more to make your dreams a reality. In the end, your thoughts will determine your actions and therefore your reality.

Key Lessons:

To achieve your goal, it's essential to create an empowering mindset. Below are a few ways you can do this.

1. **Choose thoughts that serve you:** Focus on empowering thoughts that keep you in a positive emotional state and encourage inspired action.
2. **Become a full-blown optimist:** Remove negativity from your life and focus on the positive side of things. Let go of all the petty worries you can't do anything about. Remember, 92% of your worries are useless.
3. **Visualize your goals:** Empower your subconscious mind by visualizing your goals repeatedly. Feel as though you've achieved your goals and practice moving through your day with confidence.

* * *

Action step

Do the exercises in the workbook. (*Section III. 7b. Creating the right mindset.*)

* * *

4

OTHER KEY CONSIDERATIONS

In this section, I'll cover some more issues that are crucial to consider when setting goals. I'll discuss topics like the pros and cons of sharing your goals, how to create accountability, the importance of being flexible with your goals, and whether or not to abandon them.

On Sharing Your Goals

Should you share your goals?

The decision to share your goals with others is a personal one, and you must consider the pros and cons before doing so. Let's start with the benefits. Sharing your goal might be an effective way to motivate and hold yourself accountable. Sharing your goals with colleagues, family, or friends shows commitment and makes it harder for you to give up.

It might also help you make goals that are realistic and have reasonable chances of being achieved. If you consistently fail to reach your goals, your self-esteem will suffer and those you've shared them with might mock you. For this reason, you'll have a strong incentive to think carefully about your goal and ensure your deadlines are reasonable.

As I alluded to earlier, when you share your goal, be sure to use words that show confidence. The words you use have a big impact on the way you feel, so this will help your goal become a part of your reality. I've found sharing my goals with many people doesn't just motivate me, it also opens me up to new opportunities. The more you share your passion and talk about your goals, the more likely you are to meet people who can help you achieve them. But again, clarity is important. If you know exactly what you want and are truly passionate about it, people won't just want to help you, some of them might also know how to do it.

Additional tip:

When you speak of your goals, try to avoid the following words:

- Would
- Could
- Should
- Might
- Try
- Hope
- Wish
- Maybe
- Perhaps.

Use this next set of words and phrases as much as possible:

- I will
- Absolutely
- Definitely
- Of course
- Surely
- Certainly
- Obviously
- Without a doubt
- No problem.

The downside to sharing your goals

Now we're going to discuss the disadvantages of sharing your goals. Below are four pitfalls to avoid when sharing your goals.

1. Setting your goals too low: One risk is you may end up setting your goals too low to avoid being ridiculed if you fail to achieve them. .

2. Setting your goals too high: Another is setting them so high they are impossible to reach, which will erode your self-esteem and make it harder to trust yourself, if and when you fail.

3. Sticking to outdated or irrelevant goals for too long: You have to accept the fact, for various reasons, there will always be goals you don't achieve. If you commit yourself publicly to a specific goal, you might feel peer pressure to stick with it even when it's no longer important to you. This pressure might reinforce your 'why' so much, it lingers and becomes a burden, even after you've outgrown your goal. The pressure may be intense, but it shouldn't control you.

Let me give you an example from my own life. When I shared my goals on my website, I thought announcing them meant I had to accomplish all of them no matter what. As a result, I put a lot of pressure on myself and ultimately felt overwhelmed. Eventually, I realized it was impossible to accomplish everything on my list, and started refocusing on what truly mattered to me—working on my blog, researching, and writing this book.

Sharing your goals could have some negative consequences if you lose sight of what matters to you, so remember, your goals are supposed to support you. **Don't let peer pressure force you to stick to goals that have become irrelevant to you.**

4. Mistaking discussing your goals for working on them:

In one of his talks given during a TED conference, an event aiming at spreading valuable ideas all around the world, the American entrepreneur Derek Silvers explained that, according to recent studies, sharing your goals could make them less likely to happen.

When we share our goals, they tend to become part of our reality and feel almost as if they've been accomplished. This may give us instant gratification and superficially improve our present reality, but it doesn't move us closer to a successful outcome. On the contrary, this could undermine our desire to work hard to achieve them.

I believe talking about your goals can be useful if done properly, but it's important not to get too caught up in the dialogue. When you share your goals, remember to do it with the intent of building accountability, not as a way to feel good about yourself.

Things to consider when sharing goals

Sharing goals will only be useful if you take the time to think about the benefits you're trying to gain from doing it. To help you decide whether or not to share them, consider the following points:

Benefits- What kind of benefits do I hope to get from sharing my goals?

Environmental components

- **Peer pressure-** How much does peer pressure affect me? Is it likely to prevent me from dropping or modifying my goal if necessary? If yes, are the benefits of peer pressure greater than their drawbacks?
- **Support factors-** How supportive are the people with whom I want to share my goals?

Goal-related factors

- **Goal type-** Is my goal likely to change over time?
- **Goal size-** How big is my goal? - Do you have big long-term goals you know people around you will likely dismiss as "unrealistic"? If so, I recommend you break them down into short-term goals that will likely be seen reasonable before sharing.
- **Number of goals shared** - Am I sharing just one goal or a list of them? •When you share a list of goals, you feel less pressure to accomplish all of them, which makes it easier to modify the list as needed.

Remember, you can always keep a goal to yourself. I share a lot of my goals, but I keep some big ones to myself, or only share with very close friends.

Accountability partner & mastermind group

Having an accountability partner who can monitor your progress, provide motivation, and give advice might be the best way to share your goals. People hire life coaches for this very reason—they want to clarify their goals and have someone to support them in making the changes necessary to achieve them. If you want to share your goals, why not look for an accountability partner among your friends? You could even create a mastermind group, which consists of people who come together to discuss their respective goals and support each other.

When creating a mastermind group or looking for an accountability partner, make sure:

- All group members are positive people who support and believe in you. Choose people with whom you are comfortable. Avoid including negative friends. In a group like this, they will drag you down!
- You have a clear agreement from the very beginning to ensure you're all on the same page. It's advisable to make a rule that requires honest and constructive feedback, even if the feedback is not necessarily what the other person wants to hear. After all, a group that doesn't allow you to be honest with yourself and others, won't be of any use.
- All members are starting with similar levels of "success". You don't want someone to feel superior because their accomplishments are always bigger than everyone else's. Nor do you want someone to feel inferior because their accomplishments are always smaller than those of other group members.

Remember, a mastermind or accountability group should inspire and motivate both you and the other group members. It should also provide members with valuable advice and help them move forward. Though peer pressure and guilt can motivate people, it's a subpar incentive. If you find this occurring in your group, feel free to leave it. You shouldn't continue doing something that no longer serves you.

On Flexibility

Is it ever okay to abandon a goal?

If you are someone for whom keeping promises is paramount, or you tend to be stubborn once you've set your mind to something, abandoning a goal might seem unthinkable. Perhaps you feel it would hurt your pride to give up the goal, or you don't want to pass up the chance to prove yourself. Regardless, you should never lose sight of the fact goal setting is supposed to bring you closer to your dream life. It should help you achieve goals that excite you and are aligned with your life purpose and values. As personal development blogger Steve Pavlina wrote, "*If it doesn't improve your present reality, then the goal is pointless, and you may as well dump it.*"

You also have to realize, as you read new books, acquire new knowledge, meet new people, and learn more about yourself, your values may change. You may need to fine-tune your life purpose as a result.

If you realize a goal is no longer relevant, exciting, or deeply connected with your values and life purpose, don't hesitate to let it go. You aren't here to live up to other people's expectations, you don't have to prove anything to anyone, and you certainly shouldn't pursue a goal just because you've publicly committed to it.

A real-life example of flexibility

In August 2014, I created a list of goals I wished to achieve by the end of the year. As I was working towards these goals, I soon realized the list was too long. Some goals were no longer exciting, and others were actively unhelpful. Some were related to coaching, which is an area of huge interest for me. However, I became more excited about creating my blog and working on this book, both of which made sense to do before coaching. I didn't take long to realize I didn't have enough time to study coaching seriously, or coach enough people to make the experience worthwhile. I decided to postpone coaching until I would be able to do it in a way that was much more intensive and effective than I originally planned. I went through a similar experience regarding my goal of giving a seminar on personal development by the end of the year. In a more general sense, I became intensely aware of the need to spend a considerable amount of time marketing my blog, if I wanted to increase traffic. For these reasons, I refocused my efforts on my blog and postponed my other goals.

Remember, your goals should always guide you towards the life you dream of.

When stubbornness goes wrong

A certain degree of stubbornness is essential when it comes to attaining your goals, but too much can be a hindrance. Take the following example from my own life: While majoring in Japanese, my friend and I decided to challenge ourselves to take and pass level 2 of the Japanese Language Proficiency Test. We would have a year to prepare, but had only been studying Japanese for a few months at the time. As such, the test would be difficult, and we would have to spend a year studying for hours and hours each day to have a chance at passing it. My friend quickly realized this goal was not yet worthy of pursuing. He figured, quite reasonably, he could take the exam in two years rather than one. I, however, decided to go for it, and ended up spending several hours a day studying. I ultimately passed the exam, but I can't say it was worth it. I eventually wondered why I didn't wait longer to take the exam. If I had, I wouldn't have had to study as hard. Challenging ourselves is great but we need to do it for the right reasons. I was simply trying to prove I could accomplish my goal and keep my promises. In truth, the goal wasn't helping me improve my present reality, nor was it an efficient use of my time. The major take away from this story is: **goals are supposed to help you, not waste your time!**

Should I adjust my goal over time?

While working on your goals, you may come up with new ideas and encounter new perspectives or opportunities. As a result, your original goal is likely to change over time. When this happens, take the time to work out whether the new opportunity or idea is truly exciting to you. Next, ask yourself why you want to pursue the new opportunity and figure out if these reasons outweigh the desire to stick to your original plan.

When something new arises, the people around you might tell you to seize the golden opportunity. You might even rationalize it's your best option because you'll earn more money, gain more stability, or earn more recognition. If your friends were you, they would go for it. The thing is, they aren't you, and you are striving to achieve *your* goal, not theirs. When deciding whether or not to go a certain way, ask yourself, "Does it make *me* feel good?" If money, stability, or recognition are not priorities for you, you won't have the motivation to pursue a goal that offers them —because they won't really inspire you.

It's easy to forget how important it is to follow our emotions or gut feelings when making decisions in life. **Don't let social pressure dictate the goals you strive to achieve.** Listen to your emotions and adjust your goals when you feel the need.

On visualization

What if I can't visualize?

You may be thinking, "I try to visualize, but I can't." We all visualize differently. Some can see clearer pictures than others, but it doesn't matter in the end. Just think of yourself as having already accomplished your goal, whatever that may mean to you. Don't overthink it. The idea is to put yourself in a positive emotional state, one that gives you the confidence, creativity, courage, and motivation to keep working on your goal every day.

CONCLUSION

Thank you again for purchasing and reading this book. I hope it has been of help.

Setting goals is one of the best decisions you will ever make. By deciding to set clear goals, you've made the decision to take full responsibility for your life and start creating the life you truly deserve.

My sincere hope is that this book leads you to think about your life, clarify your values, and determine the direction in which you want to go. If you follow the methods outlined within these pages, you'll achieve all the goals that really matter to you and overcome the challenges you'll encounter on the road to attaining them.

I encourage you to refer to this book as often as necessary. Use it as a motivator and a tool to achieve your goals. Remember: your goals are supposed to support you. Use them as a source of inspiration and they will take you as far as you want to go, but only if you have a clear plan and take action consistently.

You will likely fail many times while setting goals. You may set long-term goals, but fail to set daily or weekly goals consistently. You may give up setting short-term goals before starting again a few months later. You may set daily goals at work while giving yourself more freedom and spontaneity in your personal life. You may end up creating your own personal goal setting method, or you may simply set a general direction while allowing yourself great flexibility. These are all fine. In the end, what matters is:

- Do your goals help you achieve a higher level of fulfillment in your life?
- Will you regret not achieving certain goals?

You've reached the end of this book so, I'm guessing you must really like it. I appreciate you reading this far! You know, as a self-published author, it is often really tough to market my book the way the big publishing houses can. So, if you could take a few minutes to leave an honest review I would really appreciate it.

Thanks so much for your support! I look forward to hearing from you very soon. Join me on Facebook by searching for:

whatispersonaldevelopment.org

Many thanks! May your goals take you to where you deserve to be.

Thibaut Meurisse

Founder of whatispersonaldevelopment.org

What do you think ?

I want to hear from you! Your thoughts and comments are important to me. If you enjoyed this book or found it useful I'd be very grateful if you'd post a short review on Amazon. Your support really does make a difference. I read all the reviews personally so that I can get your feedback and make this book even better.

Thanks again for your support!

Bibliography

Books:

Goals

- *The Jim John Guide to Goal Setting*, Jim Rohn
- *The Magic of Thinking Big,* David Schwartz, PhD
- *The One Thing, The Surprisingly Simple Truth Behind Extraordinary Results*, Gary Keller
- *Focal Point, A Proven System to Simply Your Life, Double Your Productivity, and Achieve All Your Goals,* Brian Tracy

Mastery

- *Talents is Overrated: What Really Separates World-Class Performers from Everybody Else,* Geoff Colvin

Habits

- *Habits That Stick: The Ultimate Guide to Building Powerful Habits that Stick Once and for All,* Thibaut Meurisse
- *Mini Habits: Smaller Habits, Bigger Results*, Stephen Guise
- *The Compound Effect*, Darren Hardy
- *The Willpower Instinct: How Self-Control Works, Why It Matters, and What You Can Do to Get More of It,* Kelly McGonigal PhD

Other

- *Secrets of the Millionaire Mind: Mastering the Inner Game of Wealth,* T. Harv Ecker
- *The 4-hour Workweek: Escape 9-5, Live Anywhere, and Join the New Rich*, Timothy Ferris
- *The Effective Executive*, Peter F. Drucker
- *The Sedona Method, Your Key to Lasting Happiness, Success, Peace, and Emotional Well-being,* Hale Dwoskin

Youtube videos:

Type the titles of the following videos in the YouTube search bar

- *Assumption of Your Desire*, Joseph Clough
- *Finding Your Sweet Spot to Achieve Goals*, Joseph Clough
- *Goal Setting Workshop*, Jim Rohn, host by Jeff Fire, Millionaire Team
- *How to Set Extremely Effective Goals*, Actualized.org
- *How to Set Goals: The Ultimate Step-By-Step Goal Setting Workshop*, Project Life Mastery
- *Keep Your Goals to Yourself*, Derek Sivers
- *Small Steps Create Big Leaps*, Joseph Clough
- *Super Charge Your Goals*, Joseph Clough
- *Your Depths of Visions*, Joseph Clough

Resources on Life Purpose:

How to Discover Your Life Purpose, Celestine Chua (Free ebook):

http://personalexcellence.co/free-ebooks/

The Meaning of Life: Discover Your Life Purpose, Steve Pavlina (article):

www.stevepavlina.com/blog/2005/06/the-meaning-of-life-discover-your-purpose

How to Discover Your Life Purpose in About 20 Minutes, Steve Pavlina (article):

www.stevepavlina.com/blog/2005/01/how-to-discover-your-life-purpose-in-about-20-minutes

Need some help to achieve your goals?

Hire me as a coach and I will help you achieve your goals.

More specifically we will work together to help you:

- Change your mindset and your habits
- Overcome limiting beliefs that are holding you back
- Build stronger self-esteem so that you believe in yourself and in your ability to achieve your goals
- Create an action plan and take consistent action towards your goals
- Discover your life purpose
- Stay on track with your goals long-term

To learn more contact me at thibaut.meurisse@gmail.com

Looking forward to hearing from you soon.

Thibaut Meurisse

PART II

HABITS THAT STICK

THE ULTIMATE GUIDE TO BUILDING POWERFUL HABITS THAT STICK ONCE AND FOR ALL

Your Step-By-Step Workbook

If you haven't yet, make sure you download your free workbook by clicking by entering the following URL in your browser:

http://whatispersonaldevelopment.org/life-changing-habits

If you have any difficulties downloading the workbook contact me at:

thibaut.meurisse@gmail.com

and I will send it to you as soon as possible.

INTRODUCTION

 We are what we repeatedly do. Excellence, then, is not an act, but a habit.

— WILL DURANT

I would like to start by congratulating you for buying this audiobook. Investing your money in a self-improvement audiobook shows me that you're already serious about implementing new habits in your life (and getting rid of old ones that are physically and mentally harmful). It also means that you already have a certain degree of awareness about your current habits and understand that you need to change them in order to live a more fulfilling life.

A Little Bit About Me

My name is Thibaut Meurisse. I'm originally from France, but I've been living in Japan for the past 8 years. I'm fascinated by personal development and run a blog called What Is Personal Development. During my personal development journey, I became aware of the importance of setting clear goals. Strangely enough, most people don't have clear, written goals that they're working on each day, and even fewer people have goals that fire them up in the morning. That realization is what made me write my first book, which centered on goal-setting. I wanted people to discover that « magical tool ».

I chose to write about habits because I firmly believe that what we do every day is what determines what we'll accomplish in life. Ironically, it was only after many failures that I finally got into the habit of setting goals every day. Turns out goal-setting is its own habit, and, without it, I wouldn't have written the book you're now reading.

It is my sincere hope that this audiobook will help you create solid habits that will serve you for the rest of your life. If you have any questions, feel free to contact me at thibaut.meurisse@gmail.com.

Now, let's get started!

What You'll Learn in This Book:

Within this book, you'll find a comprehensive method to assist you in forming new habits that will support you throughout your life. You won't just learn how to form new habits. You'll also learn how to overcome obstacles and mental blocks to achieve optimal levels of perseverance. This will allow you to keep pushing until you successfully incorporate these new and exciting habits into your daily routine.

This book is inspired by other famous books, so you probably won't find anything fundamentally new in it. You *will, however,* learn the most effective ways to successfully form new habits. You'll be presented with these techniques in a fresh, unique way that is easier to understand and implement. When relevant, I'll also share examples from my own life as well as other insights that I hope will make this book even more valuable to you.

This book will do the following:

- Provide you with a step-by-step method that will enable you to successfully apply new habits that you'll stick to in the long run.
- Help you unlock your potential and allow you to leverage the power of habit to achieve significantly more in life.
- Support you in getting rid of bad habits
- Assist you in increasing your productivity and happiness by

establishing powerful new habits that yield great rewards over time.
- Enable you to avoid or conquer the obstacles that come with creating new habits.
- Give a list of some of the most powerful yet simple habits to have in life.

This book is full of valuable information, but remember, how much you get out of it is largely dependent upon how committed you are to using what you learn. The ball is in your court!

I Want You To Get Results

I really hope that you'll take consistent, massive action and commit yourself to creating powerful, lifelong habits. I believe you bought this book for a specific reason: to form new habits that will change your life and get rid of all the negative habits that prevent you from becoming the person you want to be. Am I right?

Take Action

I used to be a bookworm, but over the past few years I turned myself into a massive action taker. Why? Because I care about results more so than knowledge. Don't get me wrong, I'm still reading lots of books and loving it, but I always make sure I'm taking as much action as possible each day. Knowledge is certainly power, but knowledge without action is pretty much worthless. On its own, it won't bring you any real results in your life.

I strongly believe that the information in this book is power, but *only* if you commit to taking action. That's why I went beyond the free step-by-step workbook, I also prepared a 30-Day Challenge to further support you in the process of forming new habits.

Your 30-Day Challenge

This challenge is pretty straightforward. I want you to select one habit (preferably the one that will have the most impact once you've incorporated it into your life) and commit to doing it every day for the next 30 days.

However, there are two traps that I would like to warn you of. First, resist the urge to try forming more than one habit at a time. Focus on ONE habit at a time. Otherwise, the challenge will fail. Secondly, keep in mind that simple doesn't necessarily mean easy. This challenge may seem like a piece of cake to you, but many habits that are easy to do are just as easy NOT to do. A habit is something you do every day, not something you do every other day or whenever the mood strikes you

What If You Could Predict Success?

Do you think you can tell whether someone is going to be successful 5 or 10 years from now? You can, believe it or not, and figuring it out is actually very simple. All you have to do is take a look at their typical day. Extraordinary people have extraordinary habits, while average people have average habits. There are very few exceptions to that rule, and it applies to you. So if you want to know where you're going to be in 10 or 20 years from now, look at what you did today or yesterday. As you're reading this book, ask yourself the following question: If I keep doing what I'm doing today, will I be where I want to be in 10 or 20 years from now? Be brutally honest with yourself.

I encourage you to dig deeper by asking this question for each specific goal you have. Look at your goals and ask yourself, "Will I achieve these goals if I keep on doing what I'm doing today?" You'll know the answer if you're honest enough with yourself. How confident are you about your ability to achieve your goals based on what you're currently doing? On a scale of 1 to 10, is your confidence 8 out of 10, 6 out of 10, or even 3 out of 10? If it's less than 8 out of 10, you probably don't have the daily habits that will allow you to successfully achieve your goals. Don't worry, though, this is exactly what we'll be working on in this book. Daily habits aren't necessarily hard to do, but it's VERY easy not to do them at all. That's why you bought this book in the first place, you know you need something to help you stick to your habits.

When asked what keeps you from committing to new habits, you might argue that you were busy today and couldn't do X, Y or Z for whatever reason. You might say that you'll find the time later. The truth is, you can always come up with excuses. But if what you're doing today isn't going to lead you towards a future of fulfillment, happiness and health, there's little reason to believe things will magically change later on.

How often have you heard people say, "I'll start tomorrow"? Whether they're talking about dieting, exercise, or learning a new skill, the result is usually the same. Tomorrow comes and goes but the diet, workout, or activity never starts. And the worst part is, we knew it wasn't going to happen the minute they said "I'll start tomorrow."

Never Trust Your Future Self

If you want achieve your goals, stick to the following rule: Always assume that what you're doing today is what you'll do tomorrow, next week, next month, next year, and so on and so forth. Doing this focuses your awareness on what you're doing NOW, not what you may (and most likely won't) do in the future. By living as if what you do today will determine your future (it *will*), you'll be motivated to take action in the present instead of relying on your future self to do something later.

Believing that your future self will somehow be more disciplined than your current self is a major trap. Unfortunately, it just doesn't work that way. The fact remains, however, that what your current self does today determines what your future self will do tomorrow!

If what you're doing today isn't going to lead to the future you envision for yourself, it's probably time for you to make some changes in your life. These changes are what we're going to work on together in this book. Now, let's take a deeper look at what habits are.

1

HABITS: WHAT THEY ARE AND WHY THEY'RE SO HARD TO IMPLEMENT

Our lives are largely controlled by our subconscious minds, which are in charge of running the habits we've adopted consciously or, in most cases, unconsciously over the years.

Our brains are very efficient machines that hate wasting energy. Once the brain has been conditioned to perform a certain task repeatedly, it runs primarily on auto-pilot. This is great when you learn to drive or tie your shoes, but it's not so great when you want to break a habit. It takes significant effort to change your brain's preexistent programming, and it's an uphill battle until your subconscious mind finally accepts the change. That's why it's so hard to form new habits or get rid of old ones. Your brain isn't wired for change. It likes things just the way they are.

Why Habits are Mind-Bogglingly Important

The quality of your habits will determine the quality of our life. It's what you do on a daily basis that truly matters, not what you do from time to time or when you have a sudden burst of motivation. Take a few minutes to look at your current habits. How would you describe them? Are they the habits of a successful, happy person? Or are they the habits of someone stuck in a rut?

What a Few Simple Habits Can Do For You

When it comes to habits, it's crucial to realize that even a small daily habit can have a major impact on your life if you stick with them long enough. That's why making habits is powerful yet easy to neglect. **It's no exaggeration to say that you're just a few habits away from success and happiness!** A few good habits can go a long way. On the other hand, a few bad habits like smoking, drinking, or eating unhealthy food can take a major (and even lethal) toll after a while.

The end of this book contains a list of the top 7 daily habits that will bring you the most success in life.

Why Your Success Depends On Your Daily Habits

Your daily habits determine how much you accomplish and are very closely related to your goals. Having consistent daily habits guarantees that you'll be significantly more productive and achieve more in life. Solid daily habits will make it easier to achieve long-term goals. Let's look at some good examples of how daily habits can make a huge difference in the long run:

- Writing 500 words every day will allow you to write a book every 6 months.
- Reading for 30 minutes a day will allow you to finish 200 to 300 books over a 5-year period.
- Meditating for 15 minutes every day will enhance your long-term happiness.
- Spending 5 minutes a day on gratitude exercises will also increase your overall happiness.

Why You Are Wasting Your WillPower Without Knowing It

Unfortunately willpower is a limited resource. You can either use all of your willpower and brute force your way into getting your tasks done each day, or you can invest it strategically to create new, powerful habits that will serve you for years to come. Think of habits as a return on the investment of your willpower. More specifically, **habits are returns on** the investment of willpower that has been strategically directed towards their formation. Some use their precious willpower wisely and put it towards creating one or two positive new habits, while others waste it in an attempt to create too many habits at once. Still others do absolutely nothing with their willpower, which wastes tremendous opportunities for growth. It's all up to you, but I strongly recommend the first option!

The Incredible Power of Focused Willpower

Putting your willpower towards the creation of habits will enable you to automatize many of your tasks and turn you into a well-oiled machine. Once a habit is accepted by your subconscious mind, you will need little to no willpower to maintain it every day. Think about when you first learned to drive a car, for example. Do you remember how overwhelming it was? There were so many things going on at once, all of which required your full attention. Now, however, it's become automatic, and the entire process is taken care of by your subconscious mind. In fact, there may be times when you barely remember driving to and from home, work, and other familiar places.

That's the power of the subconscious mind, and this process holds true for habits. If you apply focused willpower to a specific task every day, it's only a matter of time before it becomes automatic.

Do you think highly successful people are virtuosos or geniuses? While this is occasionally true, most people are successful simply because they developed powerful daily habits that allowed them to become extremely efficient. The good news is that you, too, can develop these habits.

If you can learn to use your willpower to form new, powerful, daily habits that will stay with you long-term, you're in for a treat. You'll experience heightened efficiency and effectiveness, in addition to significantly increasing your levels of happiness and fulfillment.

There's a lot at stake, so make sure you invest your willpower wisely each and every day.

What a Truly Outstanding Habit Really Looks Like

When you implement new habits, you want to make sure they'll have a legitimate impact on your life in the long run. Otherwise, why bother? It may be hard to figure out how much of an impact certain habits will have on your life, but it's much easier when you know what a good habit looks like. Good habits should:

- Be something you want to maintain for the rest of your life.
- Significantly impact your productivity, happiness, fulfillment, or anything else that you genuinely value.
- Support you in achieving your long-term goals.
- Be within your sweet spot. You should feel confident that you can stick to them in the long run, even when the going gets rough.
- Have a strong "why" behind them (i.e. there should be a compelling reason as to why are they're so important to you).
- Be performed at a specific time during the day or have a clear *trigger.

*See the trigger section of this book for more details.

2

BAD HABITS: WHAT THEY ARE AND HOW TO GET RID OF THEM

The habits that have the most impact on your life are often a reflection of who you *think* you are. If you do something for long enough, it becomes closely related to your identity.

For instance, many people who smoke cigarettes associate this habit with who they are as a person. They don't see themselves a person who happens to have one (or many) cigarettes each day. Rather, they see themselves as a label, and refer to themselves as a smoker. Many people who struggle with their weight fail to see themselves as a person who is carrying extra weight. They simply think of themselves as overweight. People often think of themselves as the adjectives that describe the side effects of their habits or the habit itself (think labels like 'smoker' or 'overeater').

You may be wondering how much this matters. It actually matters a lot, because it's hard to change something that is part of the way you define yourself. So, what do you do if you realize you've been defining yourself by your habits, or the results of your habits?

The first step, as silly as it may sound, is to start questioning your identity very seriously. After all, there was a time in your life when you didn't identify with these things at all, right? There was a time when you didn't even know what a cigarette tasted like, and there was probably a time in your life, however early, where you were at a weight that was healthy for you. *You* are not a smoker. You are simply someone who smokes. *You* are not fat. You are simply someone whose habits have resulted in some extra weight.

It all comes down to habits, and just as your habits caused you to smoke or gain weight, habits can cause you to stop smoking and achieve the weight that is healthiest for your body. The *real* you can't be changed that easily.

In a way, these identities are just ideas in your mind. Repetition brought them into your reality and eventually made them part (or even all) of your identity. Fortunately, it doesn't have to stay that way.

If you want to change habits that have become part of your identity, you need to figure out who you are and who you want to be. Are you the type of person who walks every day and takes the stairs instead of the escalator? Are you the type of person who doesn't smoke in the morning? Are you someone who eats sweets in moderation?

So start questioning your identity every day. Are you really the label that you've placed on yourself? What does it really mean?

What Your Bad Habits Say About You

We all have bad habits that we're trying to get rid of. Nobody is perfect and the point is not to get rid of *all* your bad habits. That's a sure way to set yourself up for failure and crush your self-esteem. When certain habits prevent you from being happy and healthy, however, it's time to change them.

The Emotions Behind Your Bad Habits

Believe it or not, all habits serve some kind of purpose. Even your worst habits provide you with some kind of emotional benefit. If they didn't you wouldn't have them, or you could drop them with ease. It's very difficult to get rid of bad habits if you don't know why you have them in the first place There may be a habit that helps you procrastinate and avoid things that you're afraid of, for instance, or one that helps you cope with stress. Most, if not all, of your bad habits are disguised attempts to escape from something in your life.

How to Get Rid of Bad Habits

Keep in mind that certain types of habits, such as those that have turned into physical addictions like alcoholism, are beyond the scope of this book. Addictions are another matter entirely. That said, I'd like to touch upon the subject of breaking habits and explain what you can do to get rid of *most* of your bad habits.

You must start by becoming more aware of the reasons behind your habits. You need to clearly identify what emotional needs they're meeting in your life.

Be Mindful of Your Habits – The Power of Awareness

I believe self-awareness is one of the most powerful ways to get rid of bad habits forever and implement new, positive ones. The fact that you bought this book proves that, to a certain extent, you're already aware of some of your habits and how they might be dragging you down.

Take some time to look at the bad habits you'd like to change. Select just one for now. Are you aware of the emotions associated with that habit? Do you see why you have this habit and why it's so hard to get rid of? Does this habit help you cope with your fears? Is it a means of escaping from something? If so, from what?

Believe That You Can

It may sound like common sense, but you have to believe that you can actually get rid of this habit. So let me ask you: do you believe you can do it? Can you honestly answer yes to that question?

Most of what happens to us in life is the result of our beliefs. Beliefs are incredible, they can be your best friend or your worst enemy. The answer to the previous question is: Yes. Yes, you can! You are more than capable of eliminating your bad habit. However bad your habit may be, there are people out there just like you who've gotten rid of the same habit. Their ability to do this was rooted in two things: believing that they could get rid of their unwanted habit, and fully committing to doing so.

100% Commitment

Are you *completely* committed to changing your habit? Really? When it comes to changing a bad habit, you have to commit to it with every fiber of your being. Does this sound obvious, too? Getting rid of a bad habit is far from easy. Chances are, you've tried unsuccessfully in the past, and you may fail again in the future. The question is: can you commit to getting rid of that bad habit despite the obstacles you may face? Can you stick to it no matter how long it takes? Can you get back up when you fail? When the going gets tough, will you stay committed to eliminating the pesky habit that's preventing you from being the person you want to be?

Can you honestly say that you'll get rid of your habit no matter what?

Take Full Responsibility

You can't be fully committed to getting rid of your bad habit unless you take responsibility for the situation you're in now. When you don't take complete responsibility for your life, you give your power away to circumstances, situations, and people. By refusing to acknowledge that you have the power to change your current situation, you give up all hope of eliminating your bad habit.

You may be drinking because you have a problem at home or at work. You may gamble excessively or play video games all day because you want to escape your day-to-day reality. Regardless of the pressures fueling these bad habits, they still come from choices you have made. As such, the commitment and decision to stop must also to come from you.

Are you currently taking responsibility for your bad habit, or are you blaming other people and things for it? If you think you're drinking because your job is stressful or things aren't going well in your relationship, you are wrong. You are the one who chooses to use alcohol to escape. It all comes down to how YOU choose to deal with the situation. Nobody is forcing you to do anything. It may be a bitter pill to swallow, but it's the truth. If you play the victim, you'll be stuck forever. Take responsibility for your life because, situations, circumstances, and people rarely change. If you want change, it has to come from within.

How to Get Rid of Most Bad Habits

Let's look at some examples of what I call "mild addictions". This term covers the kind of bad habits addressed in this book.

Let's say you're spending 3 hours a day playing videos games and you'd like to get rid of that habit. Figure out what emotional needs the games are filling? Are you using them as a way to escape your responsibilities? Do they help you deal with stress at work or in your personal life?

You could be using your bad habit as a way to procrastinate, or it could be a mild addiction related to the instant gratification that you receive from it. Television, social media, video games, and food are prime examples of these types of habits. In fact, they are largely designed to hook you in by exploiting a "biological loophole" that advertising takes full advantage of. You've probably noticed how each episode of your favorite shows end in a way that makes you obsessed with seeing the next one. And if you're like most people, you've probably found yourself binging on television shows.

When you step back and look at the big picture, however, you'll see that video games, television shows, and social media platforms that look so appealing on first glance don't really contribute to your happiness and well-being.

We're wired to respond to instant gratification in whatever form it comes. Even so, with enough commitment, awareness, and preparation, we can eradicate our bad habits. I'll explain this more in upcoming sections.

Observe Your Emotions Without Being Judgmental

What emotions do you feel before, during, and after you engage in your bad habit? Do you feel excitement right before it starts? What about during it? Is the excitement still there after it's over, or do you experience feelings of guilt or dissatisfaction? It's important that you take the time to observe your emotions during each phase without judging them. Now, let's take an in-depth, step-by-step look at these 3 phases. For simplicity's sake, let's use video games as our example.

Before

How do you feel when you get the urge to play video games? Stay with that feeling, observe it with the kind of curiosity and objectivity you would expect from a scientist. Stop yourself from acting on it just for a while. Don't try to ignore it or turn it down. Then, try to recall how you felt the last time you finished playing video games (see "After" section below). Did you feel happier, more fulfilled, or more confident?

At this point, you should tell yourself that you'll play video games in 5 minutes, but just want to do something else that you enjoy first. This could be reading a book, listening to your favorite song, or playing an instrument. It really doesn't matter what it is as long as you like the activity. The higher your chances of becoming absorbed in it, the better.

How This Helps:

- Becoming more conscious of the feelings you have when you're about to dive into your bad habit allows you to start gaining control over the situation.
- Delaying the moment you'll start engaging in your habits helps you condition to stop acting on impulse.
- Starting a different activity for a few minutes shifts your focus away from your habit, especially if the other activity is something you particularly enjoy. You can then delay the moment you start your bad habit even further whenever possible. You may even skip it altogether sometimes! As you repeat this process, you'll become be

tter and better at resisting the urge to act on your emotions.

During

Observe the emotions you feel while playing video games with the same curiosity and objectivity that we discussed above. How do you feel? Are you really enjoying the process? Or is it less pleasurable than you thought it would be?

Create multiple interruptions as you're playing by taking breaks or doing something else for just a few moments. Stop to get a drink, go to the bathroom, or tidy up your area. These interruptions can come at intervals of your choosing. You could set a timer to stop playing once every twenty minutes, or you might decide to take a break whenever your feelings about playing fluctuate. Make sure these interruptions are given a genuine effort, though. Pause the game, turn off the television, or whatever action applies, take a moment to become conscious of how you feel, then start your other activity. Try sitting or standing somewhere else, or go to another room if possible.

During this process, it's important to give yourself total permission to go back playing video games at any time. Don't blame yourself, don't try to force yourself to resist the urge to return to them. Go back to playing video games if you feel like it, or keep on with your other activity. Either one is fine.

Why it Works:

- Staying in touch with your emotions heightens your self-awareness, which leaves room for alternatives to your habit, such as taking a break or doing something else. This will make it much easier to cut back on or totally eliminate your habit, depending on which option is healthiest (remember, some things are fine in moderation).
- By turning off the TV, pausing the game, or taking a break, you interrupt the "trance", at which point you may realize that playing video games wasn't as fulfilling as you expected. As you start other activities, you may become so absorbed with them that you forget the urge to engage in your bad habit.
- Have you ever forgotten to do something you really wanted to do because you were interrupted or started doing something else? I've done this on a number of occasions, and that's exactly what we're recreating here. When you're caught up in a certain activity, it often seems as if you just can't stop. As soon as you get distracted and start doing something else, however, you break

the spell and often wonder why you were so absorbed in the previous activity.

After

Pay close attention to how you feel after you're done playing video games. Are you satisfied and happy? Or does it feel as if you wasted your time again just like yesterday and the day before it? Do you experience guilt? Stay with your feelings, whatever they may be. Then, imagine what else you could have done instead of playing video games?

Keep a time log where you write exactly how much time you engage in your bad habit. Do this for at a week, then multiply the results by 52 to figure out how much time it takes out of your year. How many hours do you spend playing video games, watching TV, gambling, etc. What else could you have done with all that time?

If your habit is something you do multiple times a day, like checking emails or going on Facebook, use an app that will record how much time you spend doing that. You can also keep a piece of paper by your computer and use it to record every time you check social media or emails. These tactics might sound simple, but they'll force you to become more conscious of your actions and take note of what you're actually doing. You might be shocked by how many times you check your emails or social media accounts each day!

<u>Why it Works:</u>

- By getting in touch with the shame, guilt, frustration, and negative feelings that come after you've engaged in your habit, you'll begin to associate the activity with pain. You'll realize that, in retrospect, it never feels as good as you think it will. Remember those painful emotions each time you're tempted. Are you sure you want to feel that again?
- Keeping a time log forces you to become more conscious of your activities and sheds light on how much time you're really spending on that not-so-fulfilling habit. It compels you to face a harsh but necessary reality.

Replace Bad Habits With Better Ones

Eliminating unsavory habits is only part of the process. It's important to understand that replacing negative habits with better and more positive ones is much more effective than simply trying to get rid of bad habits.

If you decide to stop playing video games three hours every day, what are you going to do instead? If you have no clear plan on how to use that time, you'll very likely go back to your old habits. Your brain likes the status quo, so, if you don't give it anything else to focus on, it will guide you back to playing video games.

In the previous section, I mentioned interrupting your activity to do something else you enjoy. So what was this other activity that you enjoy? Surely there's more than one. What kind of things could you do that can get wrapped up in pretty quickly? Maybe it's reading and writing? Or perhaps it's cooking? What about exercising? Chances are, you have plenty of options. Just ask yourself the following question: What activity could satisfy the emotional needs that I've been using my bad habit to cope with?

Additional Tip: Consider recording your emotions before, during, and after your bad habit for 7 days straight. This will ensure that you're doubly aware of your emotions and will increase your mindfulness.

Visualize the Future Cost of Today's Bad Habits

Can you imagine what your life will be like 20 years from now if you fail to eliminate that bad habit? When it comes to improving our lives, imagination is one of the most powerful tools we have. Our imaginations allow us to use our minds to create whatever experiences we want at any given time. You can enjoy various scenarios and situations in your mind as often as you like without spending a dime. This is why professional athletes, chess players, army generals, CEOs, and other successful people use visualization on a daily basis.

We all use visualization, even if it's on a subconscious level. The problem is that, if you're like most people, you're probably visualizing negative things. You might be worrying about the future and visualize yourself losing your job or failing an exam. You might also be dwelling on and visualizing the past.

In the exercise below, we're going to use both positive and negative visualization to help you get rid of your bad habits. I learned this exercise from Leo Gura's video on habits "Bad Habits - A Live Exercise For Dropping Any Bad Habit For Good". You can check out his video to help you through the exercise. But now, for a brief explanation of how it works:

Visualize Your Negative Habit

- Visualize yourself engaging in your bad habit throughout the day. How does it make you feel?
- Now visualize yourself doing it for the next 30 days.
- Next, imagine yourself doing it for a whole year. Imagine the disappointment of the people around you, and think of how it will negatively impact your life.
- Finally, imagine yourself 10 years from now. Visualize the habit getting stronger, as habits almost always grow stronger with time. How do you feel? Focus on the pain associated with having had this destructive habit in your life for a decade. How has it impacted your life? How would that prevent you from reaching your potential and living a truly fulfilling life?

Visualize Your Positive Habit

- Visualize your new positive habit, and imagine yourself doing it today. What feelings does this bring up?
- Now, visualize yourself sticking to this new habit for the next 30 days.
- Next, imagine engaging in this habit for an entire year. How does it affect your life? How much difference does it make? Imagine its benefits, and what it has allowed you to accomplish.
- Finally, imagine yourself 10 years down the line with the new habit still in place. How has this new habit transformed your

life? What impact has it had on those around you? How much happiness and fulfillment has it brought you?

Visualization is a very powerful tool, but it becomes increasingly effective when it's done repeatedly over long periods of time. You should try to use visualization as often as possible. If visualization is something that resonates with you, I encourage you to take a few minutes every day to go through this exercise.

The next portion of this book includes concepts from a section of my productivity book that can be applied to the making and breaking of habits. Understanding these concepts will help you find the motivation to work on the activity that will replace the habit you're trying to eliminate. Procrastination is the primary concept covered in this section, and it's the enemy of creating positive habits. Think about it. If you put off the activities that are supposed to replace your bad habits, what's going to happen? You guessed it! You'll go right back to your old habit. Bad habits die hard!

From Procrastination to Action

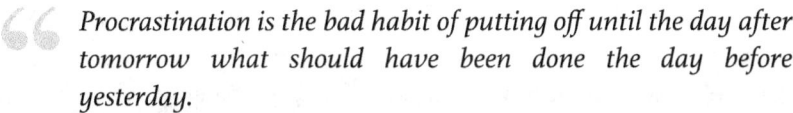

Procrastination is the bad habit of putting off until the day after tomorrow what should have been done the day before yesterday.

— NAPOLEON HILL

As I've said before, the urge to procrastinate is often strongest just as we begin to work on our most important tasks. Procrastination is a huge obstacle that can seriously limit your productivity. On one hand, you're driven by fear and a powerful urge to escape. On the other, you're really passionate about what you're trying to do and want to start working on it already.

The question is: how do you replace the paralysis of procrastination with action? It's not going to be easy, but the following three-step formula will help tremendously:

1. Eliminate Distractions

The first order of business is to leave as little room for distractions as possible. When you feel the urge to procrastinate, you'll find yourself interested in anything but your task. Stay one step ahead of distractions by identifying potential **procrastination patterns**. When are you wasting time and why? Is it procrastination or inefficient prioritizing that's draining your time?

Use the results of your time log investigation to create a **Not-To-Do List** based on the results you get from the time log and put the list on your desk. My list looks something like this:

- Don't check emails
- Don't check Facebook or other social media
- Don't go on YouTube or Google
- Don't go for a walk
- Don't check my phone
- Don't eat
- Don't check my book sales on Amazon
- Don't go to the convenience store to buy a drink

The next line of defense is removing all distractions from your desk. You should also plan your tasks in advance, prepare your environment, and give yourself a way to jot down intrusive thoughts. Keep phones, books, food, and other such items far away. The day before you start working on your task, spend some time visualizing yourself doing it. This will help you condition your mind and decrease the risk of distractions.

You can prepare your environment by readying the tools you'll need for your task ahead of time. Make sure everything is easily accessible. Do any and everything you can to make things as effortless as possible.

Last but not least, keep a piece of paper on hand in case something pops into your mind as you're working. Use it to write down any ideas or lightbulb moments that come to you. Otherwise, you'll remember something you forgot to do and decide to work on it... only to end up spending an hour on Facebook.

2. Become Aware of Your Fears and Emotions

Get in touch with the feelings that come up as you gear up to work on your task.

- Be aware of your feelings when you start working on an important task
- Use a time log to bring awareness on the way you're using your time

3. Reduce the Friction Associated with Starting the Task

It's essential to reduce the discomfort involved in beginning your task. You can accomplish this through visualization. Consider your current feelings and imagine how you'll feel once your task is completed. If that doesn't work, just start and see what happens. Tell yourself you'll only work for a few minutes. You can handle almost anything for five minutes, right?

If fear is still getting the best of you, accept the possibility that you may not do as good of a job as you'd like. Make it okay to do poorly. The reality is that you probably won't do badly unless you're extremely tired. And if you *really* think you'll do a subpar job, what makes you think you'll do any better tomorrow or next week? After all, your plan was to work on it *today*.

3

HOW TO IMPLEMENT ROCK-SOLID HABITS THAT REALLY STICK

Now that we've covered bad habits, let's move on to the exciting parts: How to implement new, positive habits that will bring great results and more fulfillment in life.

Are you ready?

Failing To Plan Is Planning To Fail

In this section we're going to talk about the importance of preparation when you implement a new habit into your life.

Mental Preparation: Getting Your Mind on Board

The most common reason we fail when attempting to build new habits or work on new goals is lack of mental preparation. If you bought this book, chances are you've tried and failed to form new habits many times in the past. Before you give it another (and might I add successful) try, you have to ask yourself exactly why your previous attempts failed. Was it because you tried to implement too many habits at once? Did you lack a strong, intrinsic motivation to break the habit? Were you trying to do it for someone else rather than yourself? Or was it hard to fully believe in yourself? These are common sources of failure, but the reason behind yours might be completely different. Take some time to refer to the workbook and reflect upon the reasons your previous attempts have failed.

Anticipate Obstacles

Now that you're clearly aware of the reasons behind your previous failures, it's time to prepare yourself mentally. To do that, you must anticipate the obstacles that may prevent you from forming your new habit and sticking to it in the long run. After all, what's the point of implementing a new habit if you drop it after a few months? Before starting your new habits, you have to take into account all the mental blocks you may have. Consider the following questions: How confident are you that you can stick to this new habit? What are some potential obstacles that could lead you to give up?

Believing in Yourself

Do you believe you can stick to your new habit? If I were to ask you on a scale of 1 to 10 how confident are you that you'll be able to stick to it for the next 30 days what would you say? If your score isn't 8 or more you might need to chunk down your habits to make it more realistic and more believable.

Now that you know where you stand regarding your new habit, can you identify all the possible reasons why you could fail?

Prepare Yourself for Obstacles

Things rarely go as planned and there are many things that may stand in your way as you try to establish new habits in your life. It's essential to take the time to identify the roadblocks you may face with as much clarity as possible. So, what challenges do you think you're likely to encounter?

Let me give you an example of what your list may look like. Let's assume your goal is to stick to your new diet, which includes reducing your sugar intake. Let's further assume you've decided to do this by breaking your habit of drinking sodas and choosing low-sugar beverages instead.

In this case, you might face the following obstacles:

- Dinner with friends, because it's difficult to eat healthy when everyone around you is eating tempting foods and drinking the sodas you are trying so hard to avoid.
- Fast-food chains, because you can easily grab unhealthy food and drinks on your way to work.
- Emotional eating, because people tend to crave sugar when stressed.
- Lack of support. If you're the only one in your family or circle of friends who's watching what they eat, it's going to be difficult. It isn't easy sticking to your habits while watching others indulge in the very things you're trying to avoid.
- A weak "why" because you know you *should* eat healthy but don't feel motivated enough to do so.

When considering these obstacles, it's a good idea to figure out what triggers you to drink soda and what you can do to work around it. You might purge your fridge of all unhealthy beverages, join a support group, or enlist your friends to help you stay on track when you're going out with them. If you've made a past attempt at a similar diet that didn't go well, you should think about why it didn't work out and see what you can learn from that experience. It's also advisable to sort through your underlying thoughts surrounding food. Perhaps you associate certain foods or even excessive eating and drinking with enjoyable activities such as going to the movies, hanging out with friends, or spending time with family. Or maybe you associate them with comfort and use them to cope with unpleasant feelings and situations. If any of these things is the case, it would be wise to adopt new beliefs that don't support these unhealthy associations and links.

Now it's your turn. What are some obstacles you're likely to encounter and how will you overcome them? How will you address each of these obstacles, and what can you do to minimize them? Take some time now to write down your answers using the downloadable worksheet.

Have a Preemptive Plan

> *Optimism can make us motivated, but a dash of pessimism can help us succeed. Research shows that predicting how and when you might be tempted to break your vow increases the chances that you will keep a resolution.*
>
> — Kelly McGonigal, The Willpower Instinct.

Now I'd like to imagine yourself in some of the scenarios you wrote down in your list of obstacles. What will you do when one of these situations arises?

By preparing yourself mentally and rehearsing how you'll deal with challenging situations in the future, you'll significantly increase your ability to resist temptation and stay on track with your goals.

In the instance of the low-sugar diet, you could visualize yourself entering a Starbucks and ordering a coffee with no sugar or another drink with a minimal amount of sugar. This may not be enough to prevent temptation entirely. It will, however, make it easier to make the right choice instead of acting on impulse. You could also visualize yourself opening the fridge and taking a bottle of water instead of a soda. As you continue to visualize yourself making healthy decisions, you'll increase your chances of successfully dealing with real-life temptation.

The "If... Then" Method

This is a highly effective approach to minimizing your chances of reverting to your old habits. In a nutshell, this method involves creating alternative to what you're trying to avoid. This drastically decreases the risk of making the wrong choice.

Example:

- If I'm out with my friends, everybody is drinking soda, and I feel a strong to order one, too, **then** I will order a coke zero instead.
- If I see a Starbucks, **then** I will cross the street.

Okay, now it's time for you to give it a go. Based on your previous list, how can you use the If...Then Method to create powerful alternatives to your bad habit?

You Are The Product Of Your Environment

We've already discussed how you can use visualization to mentally prepare yourself for coping with tempting scenarios. In this section, however, we'll go one step further by discussing how you can change your physical environment to reduce or even eliminate the obstacles on your list.

Let me start by sharing a short anecdote from my own life. I first noticed how powerful our environment is while eating nuts that I kept on my desk. I didn't even realize I was eating them until a brief moment of clarity interrupted my then-typical lack of awareness . When I discovered that I was eating nuts without even thinking about it, it made me wonder what else I might be doing unconsciously. It hit me that I would have eaten whatever was on my desk, be it chips, cookies, or carrots, without even noticing.

This simple story illustrates how much we are influenced by our environment. As someone with a sweet tooth, I would sometimes "binge" on cake and other sweets. Once I became aware of this tendency, I stopped buying sweets. If you were to come to my apartment, you'd be hard-pressed to find candy or pastries. When I happen to receive a food-related packages from my parents for Christmas, it generally results in some unhealthy "binge eating". I'll be the first to admit that this may indicate a lack of discipline on my part. But, it also shows that, when it comes to habits, minimizing temptations within your environment can go a long way.

Making strategic changes to your environment will allow you to limit the amount of willpower you expend when performing your daily habit. You don't want to leave any room for excuses and distractions, nor do you want to create unnecessarily tempting situations when you're just getting started. If, for instance, you want to replace unhealthy foods and drinks with nutritious meals and water, the last thing you want is a fridge full of chocolate milk and frozen pizzas. Having chocolate milk in plain sight might not be good idea either.

Here are a few more examples of some of the ways that you can make your environment more conducive to developing new habits:

Example 1: Keeping your home free of junk food and your workspace clear of unhealthy snacks to avoid compulsive eating. I've mentioned this before, but it bears repeating.

Example 2: Keeping your running shoes by your bed if you're trying to make a habit of going for morning runs when you wake up.

Example 3: Putting cigarettes in a place that's difficult to access if you're trying to stop smoking. Or, storing them at a friend or relative's place so that you have to ask them each time you want to smoke.

Surrounding Yourself With the Right People

Another major component of engineering a favorable environment is surrounding yourself with the right people. I once read a quote which stated the following: *If you want to lose weight you should surround yourself with skinny people.* Strange as it may sound, I've found the concept behind this quote to be very true.

I'm a firm believer of the power of surrounding yourself with people that have the kind of life you want. If your friends are all health-conscious, it's obvious that there will be fewer temptations to eat unhealthy food when you go out with them. I'm not saying you should get rid of all your friends (though in certain cases it may be necessary). What I am saying is that you should surround yourself with as many people who encourage and exemplify your goals as possible.

Now that you've mentally prepared yourself and altered your environment to support your new habit, let's look at how you can strengthen your commitment and make this new habit stick.

How Much Skin Do You Have In The Game?

Give it 100%

How often have you started something half-heartedly and wound up not getting results? The best example of this is those famous (or is it infamous?) New Year's resolutions. To be frank, I think New Year's resolutions are pretty ridiculous. I can't help but wonder why I should wait until the beginning of next year to start setting some goals and improve my life. But I digress. The main problem with New Year's resolutions is that most people who set them fail. The reason behind this is simple: People who rely on New Year's resolutions to make changes don't have clear goals. If they had monthly and yearly goals, they wouldn't need New Year's resolutions. Because they don't have a good understanding of how goal-setting actually works, their resolutions end in failure. Sadly, this isn't surprising, considering the fact what a powerful yet underused tool goal-setting is. It's so underused, in fact, that I actually wrote an entire book on it to help my readers master it.

Now, coming back to commitment, let's be honest. You can't really achieve anything if you aren't 100% devoted to it. In this section, I'll discuss some important points you need to consider when working on your new habit.

Understanding Your Why

It's difficult to be fully devoted to achieving something when you don't have a strong reason behind it. Think about some of the habits that you've tried to continually implement in the past only to fail miserably each time. We all have them. If you hate cleaning, for instance, it's going to be difficult to turn cleaning your house into a daily habit. You may understand from a logical standpoint that you should clean your place, but if you're honest with yourself, you don't really care (wait, am I talking about myself here?). My lack of excitement for cleaning aside, if a particular habit isn't all that important to you, you won't see clear benefits to it. And that is precisely why you'll fail. To avoid this, you would have to give cleaning a new meaning. Otherwise, it's not going to happen.

Should vs. Want

Now, back to the new habit you'd like to implement. What words do you use when you talk about it? If you say something along the lines of "I should do X" then there's a good chance that this is a habit you think you should adopt due to external pressure. This pressure can come from a variety of sources, such as your parents, friends, and colleagues, or even society itself. If, however, you tend to say "I *want* to do X", it's likely that it's something that means a lot to you personally. As such, it will be easier for you to rely on intrinsic motivation, which increases your chance of success.

What if My "Why" Isn't Strong?

If you discover you don't have a particularly strong "why" behind your habit, don't panic. There are ways to work around this. Going back to our previous example of wanting to tidy up on a daily basis while battling a hatred of cleaning, let's take a look at what you can do when your "why" is weak.

<u>Solution 1:</u> Use reframing to change what the task means to you.

If you don't associate cleaning with anything positive, you could train yourself to see it from a different, more positive point of view. For example, would you clean your house if you had guests coming tonight? If the answer is yes, that tells me you care what others think about the way your home looks. It also tells me that neglecting to clean your place in that circumstance would cause feelings of shame and potentially lower your self-esteem. That means cleaning your home could be seen as part of taking care of yourself and having bolstering your self-esteem. You obviously care enough about your guests to do some cleaning. Why would you do something for them that you're not willing to do for yourself? Doesn't that seem like a sign of low self-esteem? You should care enough about tidying up on a regular basis and, when you think of it this way, cleaning probably sounds a lot more appealing. The great thing is that this type of reframing can be applied to any other habit that lacks a strong "why".

Solution 2: Delegate the task.

As simple as it may sound, you could decide to delegate or outsource the task. If no amount of reframing can change the fact that you hate cleaning and see little value in it, it's probably not a wise way to use your time. Why not spend a little bit of money and hire someone to clean every once in a while? You can then invest the time you would have spent cleaning into more meaningful tasks.

Write Down Your Habit

Writing down your habits and goals is the first step to turning them into reality. I like to write both daily and long-term goals on paper. In my goal-setting book I mention in more details the benefits of writing your goals down, and how to do so effectively. For right now, however, let's focus on how to go about recording your habits.

At this point, you should have already written down the new habit you want to add to your life. If you haven't, grab a pen and paper or use the workbook to write down exactly what your new habit is. Then, write down what makes it important to you.

Ideally, you should read the "what" and "why" of your habit out loud every day to strengthen and maintain your commitment.

Have an Accountability Partner

Another powerful way to stick to your new habits is to have an accountability partner. Having an accountability partner that can monitor your progress, provide motivation, and give advice is tremendously helpful. Some people even hire life coaches for this very reason, they want someone to support them as they make positive life changes. An accountability partner can be anyone that motivates, encourages, and supports you. Feel free to consider me as your accountability partner as you go through your 30-Day-Challenge. It would be quite an honor for me.

Being held accountable by another person has another benefit: It provides a major incentive to follow-through. You don't want to have to tell someone that you didn't do what you promised you would, or that you fell off the wagon. And you certainly don't want to disappoint someone who believes in and is rooting for you.

You may want to take this benefit a step further by incorporating consequences. It could be something as simple as agreeing to give a certain amount of money to your accountability partner if you fail to stick to your habit.

Something like that is great because it forces you to ask yourself an indirect but extremely important question: How much do I believe in my ability to stick to my habit? If you're scared of betting money, then you don't fully believe in yourself. Being willing to bet money shows that you're completely committed and really believe in yourself. The more you're willing to bet, the truer this is.

So take a few moments to think about your levels of commitment and self-belief. How much money are you willing to bet that you'll stick with your new habit for the next 30 days. $10? $100? $1,000?

To further illustrate the power of commitment, let me give you a simple example from my daily life that happened to me. My dentist recently told me to start a regimen of daily exercises to correct a jaw issue. I didn't feel I had the time for the exercises and I couldn't find the motivation to do them. But I still promised her that I would do the exercises every day for a month. I even specified the time of day that I would do them. So, do you think I'm doing my exercise now? You bet I am! After all, my dentist will be able to tell whether I've done the exercises when I go to my next appointment, and I don't want to be put on the spot and forced to admit that I failed to do what I said I would. Despite my lack of enthusiasm for them, the exercises are now part of my morning ritual. This example might sound silly, but it speaks volumes about the power of accountability.

Is there anyone you have in mind for your accountability partner? It may take some time to find someone who fits the bill, but it will ultimately happen. So, let's discuss what you should do once you find the right person.

When you talk to your accountability partner, you should discuss the following:

Your habit

Talk about what your habit is (in as much detail as possible) and how the two of you will know if you've succeeded in implementing it. Decide how many days you'll commit to. Will you stick to your habit for 30 days? 60? Perhaps 90? Pin down the length of time and set a completion date.

What You're Committing To

Come up with a clear declaration of exactly what you intend to do. If, for instance, you want to start working out on a daily basis, you would say "I'm making a commitment to go to the gym every morning for the next 30 days."

Why This Habit Matters to You

Go over what you'll gain from honoring your commitment, and contemplate the consequences of failing to establish the habit.

What You Expect From One Another

This subject should be covered in great detail. Establish their wants and needs as well as your own. And, most importantly, make sure you're both on the same page regarding your partnership.

How You'll Relay Your Progress

Decide how you'll keep in touch. Some people prefer emails or text messages, others prefer phone calls, and still others prefer face-to-face communication. Pick the method of communication that's best for you both. Last but not least, determine how often you'll update them on your progress.

Consequences

Figure out what will happen if you succeed or fail. Will there be rewards for your success, and if so, what will they be? What about penalties? Reneging on your commitment could mean giving a set amount of money to your activity partner, or there might be something else that serves as a disincentive to giving up.

An Extra Tip: Consider sending a daily email or text message to your accountability partner after engaging in your habit. How's that for commitment?

It's essential to be as specific as possible about the arrangement. And whatever you do, make sure your accountability partner is someone who understands the importance of your new habit and takes it as seriously as you do.

Join a Support Group

Support groups are yet another great tool. As I've said before, it is absolutely crucial that you surround yourself with people that will encourage you to achieve your goal. Being part of a group of people whose objectives are similar to yours will certainly help you tremendously. If your daily habit is part of a larger goal, joining a support group is one of the best things you can do. Can you think of a group you could join that would support your new habit? If not, the internet is a great place to start. There are forums dedicated to self-improvement and changing your habits. There are also meetups for people interested in forming new habits, as well as meetups for people that are already engaging in a specific habit (such as jogging, meditating, or running). You may not have many people in your life who are focused on self-improvement, but meeting others who are trying to build new habits is easier than you think!

Be Willing to Invest in Yourself

If you're genuinely committed to make changes in your life, you should be willing to put a little money towards it. If your habit is your habit is truly important, you'll probably be willing to put quite a bit of money towards it. Imagine if you had paid $200 for this book. How much more committed do you think you would be? It's highly likely that you would be determined to get the most out of it. No one wants to waste money, especially large sums of it.

As such, you can use money as an incentive to stick to your goals. If you've been consistently struggling to adopt a new habit, you can increase your level of commitment by investing in something to help you, whether it's a book, course, therapist, or coach. I've purchased some great resources over the years, and they've served as powerful incentives to push through obstacles and make the changes I desire.

More specifically, I tried many times to implement a daily morning ritual. I knew it would help me start my day on a good note and maintain a positive mindset. I wanted it to include things like setting my goals for the day, meditating, repeating positive affirmations, performing gratitude exercises. However, I failed miserably. And repeatedly. I finally wound up investing in a program to help me create and stick to my morning ritual. I spent $37, but I've maintained my new morning ritual for several months now and feel confident that I will continue to do so for years to come. The investment was more than worth it!

I'm a strong believer in investing in structured programs rather than wasting time trying to compile scattered information that may or may not give you results. It's often very time-consuming and exhausting, to say nothing of how difficult it is to verify the accuracy of what you find. As a result, I invest as much money in myself as I can, and I highly recommend you do the same.

Your 30-Day Challenge

What could be better than a 30-Day Challenge to strengthen your commitment to your new habit? My goal is to help you get through the challenge, and the workbook is one of multiple ways in which I will support you throughout this challenge. Consider me an accountability partner, if you will. Remember, you can have more than one!

At this point, you've gotten a lot of information about the dos and don'ts of creating new habits and sticking to them. Now it's time to start putting what you're learning into action. Are you ready to embark on the 30-Day Challenge? The fact that you're still reading tells me that you are!

If you want, you can send me an email at thibaut.meurisse@gmail.com with a simple "YES" or (better yet!) with a "YES" AND a description of what you're committing to. I'm more than happy to act as your accountability partner, and look forward to hearing from you very soon!

Execute Like A Champion

Just Get Started: The Power of Tiny Habits

Sometimes the habits you want to implement in your life seem so challenging that you don't know where to start. Remember, it's EXTREMELY important that you believe in your ability to consistently implement your new habit. This kind of belief can be a struggle for many of us, but starting small is a great way to work around it. If your new habit feels too overwhelming, try a smaller, modified version of it that feels manageable to you.

Tiny Habits are very powerful and have multiple benefits. Even the simplest habits are easy to neglect. By enabling you to lower the bar to a level that's more comfortable, Tiny Habits make it much easier to ensure you take consistent action. They also decrease the amount of willpower you have to use to implement the habit. Our brains don't like change and our minds love efficiency, minimizing the use of willpower is a wonderful thing.

Consistency Over Intensity

If there's only one thing you remember from this book it should be the fact that **consistency is far more important than intensity.**

If your habit requires so much energy that you can't sustain it long enough for it to become automatic and ingrained in your subconscious, you'll be very unlikely to succeed in implementing it. You run the risk of crashing and burning, and the harder the task is the more you are likely to procrastinate. This is yet another area where Tiny Habits come in handy.

Below are examples of Tiny Habits that you can incorporate into your life without exhausting yourself:

- **Name:** The Running Habit
- **How to Do It:** Just put your shoes on and go.

- **Name:** The Push-up Habit
- **How to Do It:** Do a push-up. And yes, I mean 'a' push-up. Just one.

- **Name:** The Writing Habit
- **What to Do:** Open whatever you use to create documents and start writing something. It can be anything you want, as long as you're writing.

- **Name:** The Diet Habit
- **What to Do:** Eat an apple. They say an apple a day keeps the doctor away (and what if they're right?)

- **Name:** Setting daily written goals
- **What to Do:** Write one simple goal and achieve it.

Is the habit you're currently trying to implement a challenging one? If so, how could you make easier to get started? Think of a way to turn it into a smaller, more manageable habit.

I did this with meditation not too long ago. I really wanted to get back into it, but I knew that diving into it headfirst would probably be too intense. I made it easier by working it into my morning ritual and starting with just 3 minutes. It's been about 2 weeks and I'm already up to 9 minutes. See how daunting things can become totally doable just by scaling them down a bit?

You may be wondering whether you should scale things back and start smaller. That's a good question, and the answer will vary from person to person. That said, the following question will help you figure out what's right for you: Will you be able to perform your habit every day for the next 30 days even when you're tired or extremely busy? If the answer is yes, you're golden. If not, then you need to consider modifying your habit until you can say yes to that question.

Never Skip Twice

New habits are very easy to skip and you might think that it isn't a big deal. However, nothing could be farther from the truth. There are many people who say that skipping a new habit twice in a row has a devastating effect on your ability to stick with it. I've had more than one habit fade away after skipping it twice, and I've seen the same thing happen to other people on multiple occasions (New Year's resolutions, anyone?). Considering how hard it can be to make a new habit automatic, I would say the Two Skips Phenomenon is very real. Unless the habit is a well-established part of your subconscious, skipping it twice in a row comes with major risks, none of which are worth taking.

As harmless as two skips may seem, its dangers make a lot of sense if you really think about it. Skipping a fresh habit twice sends a signal to your brain that the habit isn't that important after all. If skipping it twice is okay, it must be pretty insignificant.

Remember, your brain doesn't like change. It's geared towards efficiency, which can make it lazy in a way. It likes to keep things automated and predictable. Disrupting this is hard enough, don't make it worse by sending it mixed signals about whether your habit is important. When that happens, your brain will ultimately view the habit as irrelevant and sabotage your efforts to work it into your life.

Want to know the best way to keep yourself from skipping a habit twice? Don't even skip it once!

Prepare a Contingency Plan

While it's best to never skip your habit, sometimes that's easier said than done. Nobody is perfect. We can't get around the fact that you very well may skip your habit at some point. What we can do, however, is anticipate this issue and combat it with a contingency plan. If you do wind up skipping a habit, the contingency plan will get you back on track. Let's say your habit is 15 minutes of meditation every morning. If you wake up late one morning and don't have time to meditate, you can decide to do it as soon as you come home from work.

You should always be honest with yourself and have a clear reason as to why you're skipping your habit. More importantly, you should identify likely obstacles and prepare an IF... THEN plan in advance.

I Suck. So What?

As Tynan mentioned in his book *Superhuman by Habit*, it's better to do poorly at something than it is to just skip it. It's better to perform your tasks and push through fatigue than it is to skip it and rest. You might not do so well at them, but it's still much better than doing nothing.

Lack of consistency is one of the main reasons we end up quitting our new habits. There will be days were you really feel tired and don't feel like doing anything. There may be days when you want to procrastinate because you're afraid of failing. In these moments, it's best to get started anyway. Give yourself the permission to suck at what you're doing if that's what it takes for you to get it done. Just tell yourself that you'll give it a shot for a few minutes and see what happens. More often than not, the momentum gained by starting your task will allow you to accomplish more than you expect. If you're haunted by fears of doing a bad job, just take a deep breath and say, "I suck. So what?" Then carry on and tackle that task, knowing that whatever you do is a step forward, regardless of how well you do it.

Don't Blame Yourself

Sometimes it's tempting to blame yourself for skipping your habit, but that won't help you succeed at implementing it. In fact, it's one of the many tricks your mind will use to make you give up on your new habit. Your brain is lazy and will be more than happy to give up that new habit and go back to "normal". Don't fall for that! Remember, consistency is key. If you happen to skip a habit once, make sure you don't skip it the next day. Do it poorly if you need to. But whatever you do, don't lose your momentum. If you can manage that, you'll be just fine.

To help you here is a quote on self-compassion from the book *The Willpower Instinct* by Kelly McGonigal. I found it to be quite true.

"When we do experience setbacks – which we will – we need to forgive those failures, and not use them as an excuse to give in or give up. When it comes to increasing self-control, self-compassion is a far better strategy than beating ourselves up."-Kelly McGonigal

Actions Vs. Results: What Really Matters?

Have you ever felt that you weren't good enough? If so, you're definitely not alone. Almost everyone feels or has felt that way at some point. This is actually one of the main reasons we procrastinate and fail to take consistent action. We're afraid of being inept and unable to do a good job. If your new habit is challenging, you may be afraid that you won't perform as well as you'd like to. This is especially true if you're a perfectionist.

Unfortunately, most societies and school systems condition us to be result-oriented rather than process-oriented. As children, we are praised for our accomplishments, whether it's learning to walk, getting good grades, or winning a sports game.

This may not seem particularly harmful, but there's actually a major problem with it. This approach teaches us that it's the end result that counts, not the actions that led to it.

In reality, the reverse is true. The process matters much more than the result. Our brain is such an incredible machine that, if you keep taking the right actions, it will eventually figure things out. Your brain will learn through "failures" and a process of trial-and-error until you finally get the results you want. If you can keep trying until you get what you want and take each so-called failure as a learning experience, you'll be build more strength and confidence than you ever imagined. After all, being conditioned to focus on results is the reason we're so afraid of failing.

For clarity's sake, let's take a look at a real-life example of what I'm talking about. Let's say you're a blogger and you've decided to write 500 words each day. If you're writing just to write, 500 words isn't much, but you're probably writing with a specific objective in mind. Maybe you're in the process of writing a book. Or perhaps you have a great idea for a blog post and want to produce high-quality work that will have a real impact on your readers.

It's easy to imagine why you'd be tempted to procrastinate in this situation. You might worry that what you write won't be good enough for your readers, or that your book will get rejected by publishers. These fears may be crippling enough to stop you in your tracks.

You don't have to be ruled by fear, however. You can overcome it by shifting your focus. Instead of worrying about the end result of your labors (writing great content or getting published), focus on taking the right action. In this case, the right action is pretty simple: Just sit at your desk and starting typing until you reach 500 words.

Taking the right action means doing what you know is right regardless of the outcome. You know that you want to write 500 words every day. That is your right action. What sounds worse: writing something that's less than your best, or doing nothing because you're scared, tired, or uninspired? Are you going to wait until you think you can write something phenomenal, or are you just going to get started anyway?

You'll come to find that you're better off doing something than nothing, even if what you do doesn't turn out that well. We learn by doing, not by procrastinating.

Extra Tip: Erase the traditional definition of failure from your mind. What many people see as failure is actually feedback. It's a learning opportunity, an unavoidable stepping stone on the path to mastery and success. Failure goes hand in hand with success. Make no mistake however, failure is real. Fortunately, there are only two things that can lead you to true failure: Never trying or failing to learn from your mistakes. The good news is that these things are choices, and it's completely within your power not to avoid them.

The Power of the Right Action Framework

If you understand it well and practice it regularly, The Right Action Framework (the method of focusing on actions rather than results) is an extremely powerful tool. It allows you to take action while decreasing your anxiety about the results. The Right Mind Framework redefines the notion of failure, but it also redefines the notion of success. This framework defines success as taking the right action, NOT as getting results. Getting results without taking the right action doesn't qualify as success. If you succeed via luck, doing something that goes against your right action, or engaging unethical behavior, your success would be invalidated by your flawed process.

In a nutshell, true failure means not taking action, taking the wrong action, or neglecting to learn from your mistakes.

Tips: Take a moment to reward yourself each time you take the right action. That will train your mind to focus on the process of taking action rather than on the results.

Procrastination? What's that?

Okay, you're now armed with several tools. Let's take a look at them:

- Having a strong why (Should vs. Want)
- Starting super small (Tiny Habits)
- Accepting a flawed performance (I suck so what?)
- Avoiding self-blame
- Taking the right action

So what excuses do you have left to procrastinate or skip your habits? Not many, right?

The 21-Day Myth

How much time do you really need until your new habits are fully transferred to your subconscious mind? You may be familiar with the famous "It takes 21 days to form a new habit" theory, but I think that's mostly BS. Believing in it can be very counterproductive. In reality, everybody is different, and the amount of time it takes for a habit to become automatic varies from person to person.

According to a 2009 study on habits published in the *European Journal of Social Psychology*, it took an average of 66 days for participants to fully adopt a new habit. But, of course, this is an average based on the varying results of multiple people. So how much time will it take you to form your new habits?

The answer is: Nobody knows. It could take 3 weeks or several months, but it doesn't matter in the end. A habit is, by definition, something you want to do every day for years to come, so there's no need to worry about how long it will take to fully assimilate it. You have plenty of time!

If you hold yourself to the 21-day rule, you'll probably get pretty discouraged if you're still struggling after three weeks. You might feel like you're abnormal and ultimately quit your habit. **Forget about the 21 days. Consider the fact that it may take longer than that, and stay consistent with your habits each and every day.**

How fast you form a new habit depends on the following 4 factors:

1. Your specific situation.
2. How challenging the new habit is.
3. The strength of your "why".
4. Your level of motivation.

Identify Your High-Leverage Habits

Changing just one habit in your life can create great results long-term, particularly because new habits have a strong effect on current habits. If you change your habits strategically, you can maximize the amount of positive change you experience.

Think of it this way: If you make going to bed early a habit, you may find yourself meditating, exercising, or working on your side business in the morning. The increased energy that comes from getting more rest will positively impact your productivity, mood, and ability to follow-through with preexistent habits. This holds true for any new habit; it tends to make it easier to stick to the ones you already have.

Now take a look at your current habits. Are there any pivotal habits around which many others are revolving? What is the one habit that, if implemented, would have the most positive impact on your life?

Setting Up Triggers

You may be wondering about when and how to schedule your habits. Since consistency is the cornerstone of developing your new habit, you want to schedule it in a way that minimizes your risk of skipping it. The best way to do that is to set up a trigger for that specific habit. By anchoring your habit around a specific daily event, you make it easier to create an automatic pattern and ensure consistency.

There are a variety of potential triggers you can use. For instance, you could choose to engage in your habit after your shower or as soon as you wake up.

Choose a Rock-solid Trigger

The most effective triggers are things that you do every day at the same time, such as having breakfast, brushing your teeth, or walking your pet. If your trigger is weak, you're already shooting yourself in the foot. If the trigger is eating breakfast, but you don't always have a morning meal, you're going to have trouble staying on track with your habit.

Act AFTER Your Trigger

It's better to perform your new habit after the trigger and not before it. This makes it easier for you to remember. Let's say you've chosen showering as a trigger for meditation. If you try to meditate before your showers you'll tend to think, "Oh, I almost forgot, it's meditation time" (which we all know can easily lead to just plain forgetting meditation time). If you do it after your showers however, you'll think something along the lines of "I'm done with my shower, so now it's meditation time."

Make a List of Triggers

Make a list of the tasks you do 7 days a week. This list shouldn't be very long. Now ask yourself: What would be the best trigger for my habit? Let's say you want to meditate every day. Going back to the meditation example, is it better to do it as soon as you wake up? Would you prefer to do it after you take a shower? Or maybe you'd rather do it after breakfast? Choose the trigger gives you the best possible change of sticking to your habit.

Creating Series of Habits

Once you've successfully implemented your first habit, you can go bigger and create a series of habits. A chain of habits is just multiple habits that occur one after the other. You complete one, and then start the next. By repeating this process you can create powerful series of habits that will help you make positive changes in your life. This offers many benefits, and creates clear patterns that will become automatic over time.

Let's say I've been meditating consistently for the past 2 months and want to start writing my goals down on a daily basis. I would simply add that habit into my life with my meditation practice as its trigger and voila: I'd have a budding series of habits. I'd add a third habit once the second one became solid, and keep going from there. I would eventually have a strong chain to lean on.

A Potential Pitfall

If used effectively, a series of habits is very powerful. That said, it's absolutely crucial to ensure that your current habit is strong enough to support the addition of another one. If you have a series of 5 habits, but most of them are pretty new, you could end up skipping one or two and ultimately destroy them all.

Series of Habits Example

A morning ritual is an excellent example of a typical series of habits. A morning ritual is simply a succession of habits that ensure you start your morning in a positive way that sets you up for a successful day. Most successful people have some kind of morning ritual.

Here is a list of activities that might be included in a morning ritual:

- Meditating.
- Walking/running/stretching, etc.
- Setting daily goals.
- Doing gratitude exercises.
- Reciting positive affirmations.
- Reading books.
- Watching motivational videos.
- Eating a healthy breakfast.

Do you have a morning ritual? If not, I highly recommend creating one. It's one of the most effective way to ensure you stay consistent with your habits. It also allows you to leverage your series of habits. If you commit to sticking with your morning ritual, you'll be able to maintain your habits for as long as you want.

Morning rituals are adaptable, so you can tweak yours when necessary to increase its effectiveness and tailor it to your needs. If reciting affirmations is part of your morning ritual, for instance, you can modify the affirmations as your goals evolve. **Example:** As I write this book, I could design my morning ritual around my goal of completing it. Affirmations should remind you of what excites you about what you're doing. In this example, my affirmations would be linked to my current goal, and would include the following statements, or something similar:

- I'm excited about writing an incredible book that will impact the lives of thousands of people around the world.
- I'm excited about creating great books that will inspire thousands of people to set goals, find their passion, and attain the career of their dreams.
- I'm excited about writing content that will enable thousands of people to positively impact those around them and society as a whole.

The affirmations you use are totally up to. As you go through the process you'll find affirmations that will resonate with you and strengthen your "why". What does and doesn't resonate can change over time, but your morning rituals are wonderfully malleable.

If you ever struggle to find affirmations that speak to you, ask yourself why you're doing what you're doing. In this case, I would ask myself why I'm writing this book and what makes it so important? Ask these questions until you find answers that inspire you.

Later on, you might want to change your affirmations if you decide to shift your focus to a different area of your life. Going back to our example, I might decide to concentrate on eliminating harmful beliefs and realize that I hold limiting beliefs regarding money* that are preventing me from reaching my ideal income. I could then use my morning ritual as a way to overcome these limiting beliefs. I could recite affirmations on wealth or read books about building wealth to help me shift my mindset. Or I could do some money-related exercises to dig deep and get to the root of the negative belief.

Interestingly enough, creating my morning ritual wasn't easy. Writing books on habits and goal-setting doesn't mean that I have a magical superpower that enables me to effortlessly form new habits, but I wish it did! As I mentioned in the section on investing money, I failed many times in my attempt to create a morning ritual. I had watched videos about it, I understood the concept, and I even knew what kind of habits I could incorporate into it. Yet I continued to fail until I purchased a program to help me stick to it.

What about you? What series of habits would you like to create in the future? What would your ideal morning ritual look like?

Examples of Morning Rituals

As we discussed earlier, most successful people have some kind of morning rituals. Why? Because it is very difficult to be successful if you don't set yourself up for it on a daily basis. Some people start their day eating unhealthy food and watching the news, passively absorbing negativity and slowly diminishing their health. But successful people are proactive. They decide how they want to feel and what they want to accomplish throughout the day. They set their goals for the day, practice gratitude, and ask themselves powerful questions.

For instance, Benjamin Franklin would start every morning with a seemingly simple question: "What good shall I do this day?" Brian Tracy reads inspirational books for 30 to 60 minutes each morning before setting his goals. How about you? Are you reactive or are you proactive? Do you choose how you want to feel every morning, or do you simply react to your environment? Are you the type of person who is hits the snooze button several times, rushes to get ready, grabs a coffee on the way to work and hopes for the best? Or are you the type of person who meditates, exercises, and sets clear goals for the day?

Let's take a look at the morning rituals of some very successful people.

Tony Robbins

Tony Robbins is quite possibly the most famous coach and motivational speaker in the world. Here's what his morning ritual looks like:

1. Jump into a cold pool or use whole body cryotherapy.
2. Do some breathing exercises.
3. Express gratitude. He picks 3 things he's grateful for, making sure his list includes one very small thing like the wind on his face.
4. Pray for strength and wish good things for his family, friends, and clients.

Kenneth Chenault, CEO of American Express

Chenault's ritual centers around goal-setting. Before leaving the office, the last thing he does is to write down the top three things he wants to accomplish the next day. He then uses this list to start the following day.

Steve Jobs

His morning ritual centered around asking powerful questions. He detailed it in the following quote:

"For the past 33 years, I have looked in the mirror every morning and asked myself: 'If today were the last day of my life, would I want to do what I am about to do today?'

And whenever the answer has been 'No' for too many days in a row, I know I need to change something."

The 7 Most Powerful (Yet Simple) Habits To Have In Life

In this section, I'd like to provide you with what I believe are some of the most powerful habits that you can have. These habits will have a profound impact in your life in the long run. This short list is far from being exhaustive, but it will give you some ideas for future habits you might want to incorporate into your daily life.

#1 Setting daily goals.

Setting your goals every single day will, from my own experience, double (if not triple!) your productivity. To set your goals, just take a pen and a piece of paper (avoid typing on the computer) and make a list of 3 to 5 tasks you want to accomplish for the day. Then, prioritize your tasks by numbering them in order of importance. Start working on your first task until you complete it and move to the next one. Repeat the process. If you can do this on a daily basis you're bound to get a lot done. To learn more about this process, feel free to refer to my goal-setting book.

#2 Reading your goals every day.

This is a powerful way to ensure that you stay on track with your goals. Ideally, you should think of your goals as often as possible. When things get busy, it's very easy to forget about our goals, but reading them out loud on a daily basis can prevent that from happening. You shouldn't just read your goals, however, you should also ask yourself why they're so important. There has to be a strong reason behind your goals if you're going to successfully work on them. If, for instance, my goal is to earn $600 a month from my books, I'd need to state this in a way that reminds me of why this goal matters to me. I would say, "By December 31st 2016, I'll be earning $600 per month from Kindle Publishing and impacting the lives of thousands of people around the world." I could also say "By

December 31st 2016, I'll be earning $600 per month from Kindle Publishing and inspiring thousands of people to set goals, change their habits, and become role models for those around them." It's equally important to take a moment to visualize your goals and how achieving them would feel.

#3 Meditating

Meditation provides a plethora of benefits. I won't go through them all, but you can check out this http://liveanddare.com/benefits-of-meditation/ if you want learn more about them. It mentions over 76 scientific benefits!

You can begin with just a few minutes a day. There are many ways to meditate, but it can be as simple as closing your eyes and focusing on your breath. There are also several good books for beginners that can help you get started.

#4 Practicing gratitude.

Forgetting to express gratitude is a major cause of unhappiness for many of us. We take everything for granted and don't fully appreciate the little things in life (or even the big ones). There's a hilarious comedy sketch from Louis CK about airplanes and the way people take technology for granted that illustrates this perfectly. Check it out below.

> *It was the worst day of my life. First of all, we didn't board for twenty minutes, and then we get on the plane and they made us sit there on the runway...' Oh really, what happened next? Did you fly through the air incredibly, like a bird? Did you partake in the miracle of human flight you non-contributing zero?! You're flying! It's amazing! Everybody on every plane should just constantly be going: 'Oh my God! Wow!' You're flying! You're sitting in a chair, in the sky!*
>
> — Louis CK

Every day during my morning ritual, I ask myself what I'm grateful for. I then spend a few minutes thinking about everything that crosses my mind. You don't have to come up with anything major, it's okay to think about the little things. The following list will make it easier to practice gratitude by reminding you of some basic things you can be grateful for:

- Amazon, YouTube, and other such platforms that provide access to an endless supply of knowledge at little to no cost.
- Living in one of history's most exciting time periods. Kids will study our time period a thousand years from now and be amazed at the rapid increases in technology. We've gone from telegrams and carriages to race cars, camera phones, internet access, and virtual reality (among other amazing things) in less than 150 years. It's incredible!
- Having food, shelter, running water, and electricity.
- Having a phone that enables you to communicate with your friends and family no matter how far apart you are.

The list is endless!

I say what I'm grateful for out loud, but some people prefer creating a written gratitude list. The trick is to feel genuine gratitude as you contemplate the things on your list. As Jim Rohn says, "Our emotions need to be as educated as our intellect." So be patient and stick with this habit. I can guarantee it will pay off in the long-run.

#5 Consuming motivational books and videos.

In the words of Zig Ziglar, "People often say that motivation doesn't last. Well, neither does bathing – that's why we recommend it daily." No matter how exciting your goals may be, there will be time where you won't feel like doing anything.

Feeding your mind with inspirational material on a daily basis will help you stay motivated for the long-haul. If you can't find the time to read, you can also listen to uplifting audiobooks. In fact, I have a Jim Rohn audiobook that I've listened to over 100 times.

#6 Self-reflecting.

Taking a few minutes to reflect upon your day is a very effective way to improve yourself. Self-reflection is one of the best ways to supercharge your growth. When you analyze the events of your day, consider asking yourself the following questions:

- What did I do well today?

- What could I have done better?

- What can I learn from today?

- What will I do differently in the future?

#7 Exercising daily.

You already know that you should get some exercise each day, so I'm not going to try to convince you. These days, most of us spend too much time sitting down and looking at our televisions or computers.

According to Dr. James Levine, author of *Get Up! Why your Chair is Killing You and What You Can Do About It*, for every hour that you spend sitting cuts off 3 hours of your life. I haven't read this book yet, but I plan to check it out soon.

I might even invest in a treadmill desk or at least a standing desk. Did you know that some desks allow you to switch between standing and sitting with just one touch? Sounds pretty cool! So, what kind of exercise are you going to do each day?

Take Action Right Now Or Else...

I have one question for you: Have you started to take action and implement a new, powerful habit in your life? If, not will you?

Will you be the person who sets goals, finds their passion, creates a fulfilling career, and becomes an inspiration to those around them? It would be a great honor for me to have helped you form positive, life-changing habits in some way, and I would love to hear from you regarding your progress.

After releasing my book on goal setting, I received comments from people who told me that it made a real impact on their lives. These people put the book's contents to use and turned the knowledge they received into tangible result. To my delight, one of my readers took immediate action upon reading my book.

"I myself have a lofty goal that I have only just begun to work on, and after reading this book I stopped everything and used the steps to lay out a plan for not only how I am going to accomplish this, but when." – Mark Richmond, US

Another reader began to immediately impact others by sharing the book with her kids.

"Your book has been an inspiration in my life and I want to thank you. I'm halfway through your book and I want to give to my kids as well. – Kelly D.

It goes without saying that I would love to hear more stories like that from my readers.

On the other hand, a colleague who knew of my book asked to have a look at it after spotting a Kindle in my bag. I said yes and, as she looked over it, I suggested she buy it because it was on sale for just $1 at the time. $1 doesn't seem likely to break the bank, does it? Even so, she said, "I'll think about it" in a very serious tone. For those who don't know, "I'll think about it" almost always means NO in Japan.

So who do you want to be, the person who invests in themselves and gets results, or the person who doesn't value themselves enough to invest in resources that will help them reach their goals?

Your Habit Formation Checklist

We covered a lot in this book, and I would like to briefly summarize the steps you need to follow when implementing a new habit in your life.

PREPARE YOURSELF AND YOUR ENVIRONMENT

- **Select a high-impact habit** that will produce the greatest results in your life.
- **Make a list of all obstacles** that could make you give up on that habit.
- **Design a supportive environment** for your habit (make it as easy as possible by removing or minimizing your obstacles).

STRENGTHEN YOUR COMMITMENT

- Make a real commitment to yourself- Give it 100%.
- **Make sure you have a strong "why"**—Is it something you **want** or something you believe you **should** do?
- **Find an accountability partner or group**—It makes it easier to stay committed.
- **Invest your money**—Be willing to invest in books, programs, courses, or a coach if necessary.
- **Write down your habit** and why it is important to you.
- Undertake the 30-Day-Challenge.

EXECUTE

- **Select a trigger for your habit**—The trigger should be something you do every day. Make your habit easier to remember by engaging in it after the trigger, not before.
- **Start as small as you have to**—Make your habit easy to do, and assess how confident you are of your ability to stick to the habit during the next 30 days and beyond.
- **Focus on taking the right action**—Don't concentrate on results, just take the action you know is right without worrying about the results.

- **Don't blame yourself**—That's a trick of the mind designed to make you give up.
- **Don't skip your habit**—Do it poorly if you must, but always do it. Remember that skipping a habit more than once will destroy it.
- **Have an If... Then plan**—If you have no choice but to skip your habit, be aware of the reason for it and come up with an alternative (such as doing it later in the day).
- **Forget about the 21-Day myth**—Stay focused on your habit for as long as it takes to make it stick. After all, you want to be able to maintain it for years to come.

Once your habit is firmly established, work on a new one to begin the creation of a series of habits. And last but not least: always choose consistency over intensity.

Conclusion

I would like to congratulate you for staying with me until the end of this book. At this point, it's clear that your commitment is real. Now, the ball is in your court. Don't hesitate to go through this book when you need help. You may need to go over it several times as you attempt to create new habits. That's okay! If you have any question or feedback, please feel free to contact me at thibaut.meurisse@gmail.com.

Final Words

Habits are the foundation of your success. I hope you'll use the information in this book to help you create powerful new habits in your life. Creating new habits or getting rid of existing ones is never easy. In fact, I can almost guarantee that you will fail several times in the process. When this happens, it is my hope is that you will refer to this book, reread everything that applies to your situation, and try again. Habits aren't always hard to do, but they're very easy *not* to do.

What Do You Think?

I want to hear from you! Your thoughts and comments are important to me. If you enjoyed this book bundle or found it useful I'd be very grateful if you'd post a short review on Amazon. Your support really does make a difference. I read all the reviews personally so I can get your feedback and make this book even better.

Thanks again for your support!

PART III
PRODUCTIVITY BEAST
AN UNCONVENTIONAL GUIDE TO GETTING THINGS DONE

Your Step-By-Step Workbook

To help you work on your productivity I've created a step-by-step workbook. Make sure you download it by typing the following URL in your browser:

http://whatispersonaldevelopment.org/life-changing-habits

INTRODUCTION

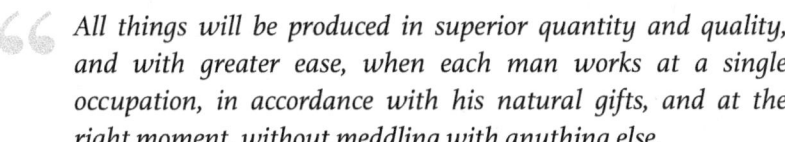 *All things will be produced in superior quantity and quality, and with greater ease, when each man works at a single occupation, in accordance with his natural gifts, and at the right moment, without meddling with anything else.*

— Plato

Do you struggle with productivity, or wish that you could get more done each day? Do you have dreams and goals that are dear to you, yet you can't imagine how to fit them into your work, family, or educational obligations? Do you procrastinate? If you're reading this book, chances are that you relate to at least one of these things. Fortunately, the information in this book will be immensely helpful for anyone who wants to increase their productivity.

Rather than simply giving you productivity methods, I will take the time to talk about what productivity truly is, and, more importantly, what it really means to you. Not what it means to someone else, but to you!

I will also spend some time explaining why you fail to be as productive as you could and what you can do about it.

What's more, I'll show you how to plan your day for maximum productivity, among other things.

What to Expect

This book will teach you the following:

- What productivity is and isn't.
- Why we aren't as productive as we'd like to be.
- How to overcome procrastination and take action.
- How to cultivate a mindset that encourages productive behaviors.
- Why you aren't really valuing your time and what you can do about it.
- How to plan your day for maximum productivity.
- How to use focus to supercharge your productivity.
- What the 1 x 1 x 1 rule is.
- How to design a productive environment

What Not to Expect

- Detailed productivity systems like the one introduced in Getting Things Done from David Allen
- Minor productivity tips, tricks or hacks

Your 30-Day Challenge

You will be given a straightforward 30-Day Challenge that will encourage you to act upon a few simple yet powerful principles mentioned in this book. This challenge represents the minimum effort that I expect from serious readers who want to make the most of their time.

THE IMPORTANCE OF PRODUCTIVITY

Without knowledge action is useless and knowledge without action is futile.

— Abu Bakr

Before reading further, you should consider how much time and energy you're willing to put towards your goals. It is also important to create a clear definition of what you hope to gain by reading this book. So let me ask you: what exactly do you want to get out of this book? Why did you buy it in the first place? Real change requires lots of inner work and drive, so let's consider several sources of motivation.

First of all, you've already shown your commitment by buying this book and I would like to take the time to congratulate you on that. You are already way ahead of most people and have partially completed your goal to increase your productivity!

Secondly, productivity is extremely important. I came to understand its importance upon the realization that I had goals that would require me to change the way I managed the hours in my day.

In fact, I have to make a confession: most of the time I don't enjoy my job.

Unfortunately, like most people, however, quitting my job to pursue my passion is not yet feasible.

That's why, for me it's vital I make an extremely effective use of my precious time in order to create an online business that I will eventually work full time on. Being extremely productive is a MUST!

The ability to get things done is what will allow me to create a successful business. While in a company you may be unproductive and go unnoticed, when you are on your own you must get results or you go broke. When I work on my business every day after work I have to be productive.

A third powerful motivator is the desire for more freedom in your life. Increasing your level of productivity means that you're now able to earn more money in less time and thus work fewer hours while enjoying more freedom to do what you want. This is probably one of the biggest motivators for me.

Finally, chances are that have you have a desire to impact your world. How well you do this is closely tied to your ability to get things done. If you can't motivate yourself to complete tasks that truly matter to you, how can you expect to influence the world?

It could even be argued that lack of productivity can become a somewhat selfish act. It prevents you from getting ideas, books, projects, or inventions out of your head that could potentially transform the lives of other people. After all, can you imagine how different the world would be if stopped procrastinating and started getting things done? How many more amazing inventions could we be benefiting from right now?

My only hope is that this book will impact you in some way and enable you to find the motivation within you to put what you'll learn here into practice. My only expectation is that you will create positive changes in your life and in the lives of those around you.

Being Productive—but at What?

Your time is limited, so don't waste it living someone else's life. Don't be trapped by dogma - which is living with the results of other people's thinking. Don't let the noise of other's opinions drown out your own inner voice. And most important, have the courage to follow your heart and intuition. They somehow already know what you truly want to become. Everything else is secondary.

— STEVE JOBS

When working on increasing your productivity it's extremely important to make sure that you pursue something you feel strongly about and genuinely want. Being productive while doing something you aren't interested in is not being productive at all! It sounds obvious, but many people spend years being productive at things they hate. If being productive at something you can't stand allows you to free up time to work towards a promotion you desire or more fulfilling career, that's one thing. Otherwise, you're wasting your time.

So, be honest with yourself. Are you being productive with the right things?

To give you an example, I consider myself quite productive outside of my job when I'm working on books and articles. Yet, when the week is over and I ask myself what I accomplished at my job, sometimes my mind goes blank. For that reason, I will eventually have to do one of the following: Quit my job, or start thinking of it in a way that better aligns it with my values and purpose in life. I'll do the former one.

In a nutshell, the first step towards working on your productivity is making sure that you are productive at something that makes sense to you, something that brings you fulfillment in life.

Here is a real-life example to illustrate what I'm talking about:

I don't know here personally but let me tell you the story of Jenna, who is a friend of a friend. Jenna knew from a young age that helping people was one of the most important things in her life. It made her feel alive, energized, and in tune with herself. She always found it easy to give compassion to difficult people and listening to the problems of others was rarely bothersome to her. As she got older, she realized that she even had a knack for helping people solve the problems they came to her with.

She had dreams of becoming a therapist, life coach, a social worker, or perhaps even a school counselor. Something that would allow her to help others and see them through life's difficulties felt fulfilling to her.

However, her father was the CEO of a lucrative company, and her mother was a doctor. She was accustomed to a high standard of living due to growing up in a high-income household, and her parents expected her to do something that would provide her with an income similar to theirs.

Certain that she couldn't bear her parents' disapproval and that a large salary would make her happy, Jenna went against her instincts and opted for a business degree. Years later, she had successfully climbed the corporate ladder to vice presidency of the company she worked for.

She earned a 6-figure salary and was considered one of the best in her field. Yet she always felt a sense of anxiety and restlessness that she couldn't shake. These feelings eventually became too much to bear, and she had to acknowledge the fact that she was unhappy with her job, and couldn't imagine spending the rest of her working years doing it.

Jenna ultimately left her job to pursue a degree in psychology. Within a few years of leaving her corporate job, she was a practicing therapist. While she didn't earn as much as she had during her corporate career, she felt happy, fulfilled, and excited to go to work each day. Her only regret was the time she wasted exchanging her happiness, contentment, and true passion for money.

<u>The point is, make sure you are productive at the right thing</u>

I find the following quotes from Steve Jobs very true:

> *You've got to find what you love. And that is as true for your work as it is for your lovers. Your work is going to fill a large part of your life, and the only way to be truly satisfied is to do what you believe is great work. And the only way to do great work is to love what you do. If you haven't found it yet, keep looking. Don't settle. As with all matters of the heart, you'll know when you find it. And, like any great*

relationship, it just gets better and better as the years roll on. So keep looking until you find it. Don't settle...

I like to listen to millionaires and billionaires as they have many great quotes. I have yet to find one who doesn't love what he or she is doing. Loving what you do will certainly help you stay productive! While finding your passion and doing what you love is beyond the scope of this book, keep it in mind and make sure your productivity is aimed at the right things. You don't want to spend the rest of your life hustling at a job you hate.

You're More Capable Than You Think

Treat a man as he is and he will remain as he is. Treat a man as he can and should be and he will become as he can and should be.

— Stephen R. Covey

If you're reading this book, you already know you want to change something in your life. If you want to make the most out of it, taking action is a must. If you read this book without taking action you won't get any results. I've learned from experience that most books, even the mediocre ones, can really make a difference in someone's life. Contrary to what most people believe, the value of any particular piece of information is often in the eye of the consumer. It is not necessarily determined by the content itself. What I mean by this is that a person who is consistently taking action will manage to get results even from average-quality books. Knowledge is power, but only when it is followed by concrete action.

Let me give you a recent example that happened just a few days ago. One of my colleagues saw that I had a Kindle in my bag and asked if she could take a look at my book on goal-setting that I had mentioned the previous day. I said yes, and, as I showed her my book, I suggested that she buy it because it was on sale for just a dollar. That price doesn't seem like it will break the bank. Even so, she said, "I'll think about it" in a very serious tone (which in Japan generally means... NO).

On the other hand, I received an email yesterday (as I'm writing this book) from a lady who asked me if my book was available in paperback. I sent her the link for it and she sent the following reply:

Thank you. Your book has been an inspiration in my life and I want to thank you. I am halfway through your book and I want to give to my kids as well.

It is entirely possible for people to value the same content very differently, and the value is directly linked to how they choose to use it.

This brings us back to the productivity workbook, which I created solely because I want you to get valuable results from this book. You can download the free workbook at http://whatispersonaldevelopment.org/life-changing-habits. It includes bonus material and some things that aren't covered in this book. It will help you through your journey. More precisely, this workbook will help you with a wide variety of issues and obstacles that come with working to achieve your goals. The workbook addresses everything from learning to value your time properly, accurately gauging your current levels of productivity, and altering self-defeating thought patterns, to increasing your focus, adjusting your priorities, and creating an environment conducive to sustainable change.

The 30-Day Challenge

> *Productivity is never an accident. It is always the result of a commitment to excellence, intelligent planning, and focused effort.*
>
> — Paul J. Meyer

It's always best to take action when your emotions are strong. This is where the 30-Day Challenge comes in. Completing the 30-Day Challenge means focusing on one goal, regardless of how many you have, selecting one major task or activity that is directly tied to achieving said goal, and performing this task or activity daily for a month

Do you often focus on too many things at once because there is so much you want to accomplish? If so, I know exactly where you are coming from. It's a very common urge. Yet I can't say enough about how important it is to focus just a few high leverage/high impact tasks if you want to be truly productive.

Achieving your goal will go from being an intangible, subjective process to something that you can take day by day. With the 30 Day Challenge, your goal will no longer be intangible. You'll be able to track your progress and cope with obstacles more easily. (From here we could go into saying that in addition to the workbook and content available on your website, they can use your earlier book for help).

If you want to set long-term goals refer to the Goal Setting book in this bundle (Part 1). In it, I detailed the exact process to follow to ensure you set exciting goals and stay on track with them.

THE DEFINITION OF PRODUCTIVITY

At this point, you have a fuller understanding of how to use this book and what you can expect from it. With that knowledge under your belt, it's time to get down to focal point of the book: productivity.

When you think about productivity, what comes to mind? What is your definition of productivity? What do you associate it with? Take some time to consider these questions. Once you've got your answers, read on to discover the definition of productivity that we'll be working with in this book. Compare your definition of productivity with the one in this book. Noting the similarities and differences will come in handy later.

The most useful definition of productivity is less complicated than you might think. Simply put, productivity is all about producing. If you want an idea of how productive you are, ask yourself the following: What am I tangibly producing right now? What will the end result of my efforts be?

Many people are task-oriented, but real productivity requires us to be result-oriented. You really want to think of yourself as a creator, someone who is creating noticeable results that have an impact. Be honest with yourself. Are you a result-oriented person? Do you frequently consider the end result of the task you're working on?

Leo Gura from *Actualized.org* likes to think of his life as a series of projects and I find the idea interesting. What are the major projects in your life right now? When exactly are their deadlines? If you don't have any clear project in your personal or professional life, you might want to look at your goals and see if what you are currently doing is producing results.

For optimal productivity, what you're doing, making, or creating needs to be important. Procrastination often appears in the form of wasting time on trivial tasks, so you should make sure that what you're devoting your time to is of significant value.

This is my personal definition of what productivity should be:

"Choosing your most impactful, valuable, and fulfilling tasks that you are best at, and applying a consistent, laser-like focus to them."

I believe this is the kind of productivity you should strive to achieve, because it focuses on two important points. The first point is making sure the tasks you're working on have a high impact. The second is ensuring that what you work on is leveraged as much as possible. Things that can be leveraged are reusable, or are scalable and can reach many people. Now, let's delve a bit deeper into all of this by defining the characteristics of productive tasks. Typically, truly productive tasks are scalable, reusable, high-impact, fulfilling, or something at which you're the best. Ideally, a productive task is all of these things. The following list further defines these characteristics.

Scalable: An example of scalability would be the book I'm currently writing, as it can reach many people via the internet and generate revenue for years to come.

Reusable: Reusable content can be something as simple as a PowerPoint presentation template or a checklist that can be reused by your company's employees, thus saving time and money.

High-Impact: If something is high-impact, it can be said that it is valuable. These tasks create massive value. No matter how great you are at what you are doing, if you aren't creating something with perceived value, you won't be all that productive.

Anyone who consumes your work must feel that what you're doing is valuable. As mentioned previously, using leverage increases the impact of the task and generates massive value. This is why it's so important to have a strong desire to impact people!

Fulfilling: Enjoying the task you're working on is a must if you want it to be fulfilling. If you can't stand the task at hand, maintaining productivity will be a major challenge, no matter how valuable the task is. Let's say you have a job involves doing research all day but you absolutely hate researching. At best, you'll trudge through it while feeling miserable every day. At worst, you'll burn out and find it hard to get much work done. Fortunately, the things you enjoy doing are usually things that you excel at. The bottom-line is this: Whenever possible, focus on tasks that bring you joy.

What You Do Best: To find out what you're best at, ask yourself the following: What is it that only I can do? Perhaps it's a task that involves high-level strategic thinking and requires extensive experience that only you may have. Or maybe it's something that is difficult for your colleagues but feels like a piece of cake to you. It is, in short, a task that you are the best person for.

This brings us to the importance of supply and demand. Although hard work and high-quality is a must, they are useless when funneled into a product for which there is no market. It's crucial to go where there is a preexistent demand. Trying to create a new market because you think your idea is awesome probably won't work. Chances are, your idea has been tried before, but failed because there was no demand for it. As millionaire mentor Dan Lok says, "Market, not marketing, is everything."

Now, can you think of ways to increase your productivity? Unfortunately, if you are currently an employee your ability to create a lot of value and reap the benefits from it will be limited. If you come up with an idea that help your company makes $100,000 dollars how much do you think you will get from it? Not much. If you are lucky, maybe a promotion. In that regards, being self-employed or having your own company offers way more room for leverage. Understand that as an employee your ability to improve your productivity will be limited.

Productivity is Not about Managing Time

Did you notice that my definition of productivity doesn't mention the word "time"? Contrary to popular belief, productivity is not really about time-management. In reality, it's more about managing your tasks. The question isn't how to manage your time so that you can complete your tasks, but rather, how to manage your tasks efficiently so that you have the necessary time to complete them. It might look like I'm saying the same thing but there is a big difference. When you focus only on managing the things that you need to get done, you're able to zero in on what truly matters and ensure that you have your priorities straight. However, you have no control over time. It passes by whether you like it or not.

True productivity can be broken down into the following 10 steps:

1. Understanding the TRUE reasons you fail to be productive.
2. Managing Your Energy
3. Valuing Your Time
4. Thinking Differently
5. Prioritizing Efficiently
6. Focusing
7. Using the Power of Leverage.
8. Creating an environment that supports productivity.
9. Planning Effectively
10. Taking significant, consistent steps towards your goals.

So, let's take a look at these steps and see how they can take you from feeling there aren't enough hours in the day to getting the results you want.

1
UNDERSTANDING THE TRUE REASONS YOU FAIL TO BE PRODUCTIVE

Most books offer productivity methods that work well on paper. Maybe you've read some of these books yourself and trying hard to use what you've read increase your productivity. Yet being productive doesn't require sophisticated methods or advanced software. These things might help a little, but they can't combat the true reason you aren't being genuinely productive.

So what's the *real* problem? Fear. Yes, fear. Fear is the *true* reason you aren't being productive. The truth is, you probably already know what you should be doing. You need to avoid distractions, complete your most important task in the morning, and follow that up with some rest before repeating the process. That is, in essence, what productivity is all about.

So, why don't you actually do any of this? If you look closely at your emotions when you're about to start an important task, you'll notice a sudden urge to check your emails, go for a walk, make coffee, or go on Facebook. You'll want to clean your home, watch a video on YouTube, dive into busywork, or (quite ironically!) read books on how to be productive! Be honest with yourself. Is that part of why you're reading this book right now? Is there anything more important that you should be doing instead?

The urge to focus on trivial tasks is driven by fear, which makes you want to run away from what you really need to be doing. This fear has a name that you've probably heard many times before: procrastination. The bad news is that it will be your biggest obstacle as you work on becoming more productive. The good news is that you can beat it.

The first step towards conquering your fear is simply noticing it. Once you see it, stay with it. Analyze it. Ask yourself what you're afraid of. Most likely, you're scared of the unknown, you're afraid that you aren't good enough, or you fear that you're incapable of doing a good job. These anxieties are what this fear is usually about. As you can see, productivity is as much about mastering your emotions as it is about implementing the right methods.

The second step is to simply get started. When you feel that strong desire to escape with distractions and excuses, tell yourself that you're just going to spend a couple of minutes on the task without any expectations. Once we start focusing on a task for a few minutes, we tend to gain momentum, and can wind up spending hours on it. With this kind of momentum, we'll probably even finish it. If your main task is something you enjoy doing, simply finding the strength to get started will often be enough. I often feel like procrastinating when writing books, but once I get started things begin to flow very quickly and I become so absorbed in what I'm doing that I can't stop writing.

Of course, there's a chance that you won't be able to focus on your task for more than a few minutes. If so, don't worry. Keep observing your fear and nudging yourself to start working on your task. If you stick with it, you'll ultimately train your mind to get things done regardless of how you feel. The fear will likely decrease over time, and, if it doesn't, you'll be able to ignore it.

What if I Still Can't Get Started?

Joseph Clough, a best-selling author and hypnotherapist, has a great way to break free of procrastination. Start by visualizing the task or project you are working on, then imagine how you would feel it you had already finished it. Do you feel relieved, thankful, or competent? Do you feel excited, happy, or confident?

Getting in touch with how you'll feel when your task is completed is very powerful. It will allow you to garner the strength and momentum necessary to start working and stop procrastinating.

Another thing that can help you get started is accepting the fact that it may not go as well as you'd like. If you can accept that you might not do well at the task at hand, you won't be so afraid to start it. No one is perfect, and you need to be okay with that. Remember: Doing a terrible job is always better than doing nothing at all. This outlook will further train your mind to choose action over procrastination.

2

MANAGING YOUR ENERGY

As we discussed earlier, time isn't what you should be managing if you want to increase your productivity. Tasks and priorities are among the most important thing to manage, but it's impossible to do this if you don't monitor your energy levels. We all have certain times of the day where we are more or less productive, depending on how energized we feel. Energy fluctuations are universal, but their patterns aren't.

Some people are night owls who do their best work in the evening, while others are morning people who focus best before noon. Many of us feel sluggish towards the afternoon, yet some get second winds during that time. Everyone is different, so it's important to observe yourself and figure out how your energy levels change throughout the day. Once you've pinpointed your pattern, you can use it to your advantage and tailor your activities to it whenever possible.

Real Life Example:

I have a preference for working on the most important item on my to-do list in the morning, as that is when my energy is highest. In addition, the act of completing something soon after the day begins provides me with a sense of momentum. I carry this with me throughout the day, and it makes it easier to accomplish the rest of the things that I need to do. If I start to feel sluggish, tired, or unmotivated, I remember that I managed to get the most difficult tasks accomplished, and suddenly whatever I'm working on becomes much simpler and easier.

On the other hand, my energy levels tend to drop after 4pm. When planning out your tasks for the day or week, ask yourself the following questions:

When do I feel the most energized? When do I do my best work? At what point during the day do I start to feel foggy or lethargic? The answers will probably come more easily than you think. In fact, if you are honest with yourself you probably already know what your natural rhythm is.

Learning to Say No

 What is the master skill of productivity? Learning to say No.

— – DARREN HARDY

Do you know what Warren Buffet response was when asked the greatest key to his success? "For every hundred great opportunities that are brought to me, I say "no" ninety-nine times."

Streamlining your commitments and learning to say no is another important part of managing your energy. In order to properly utilize your energy, you must manage your commitments. In other words, you must learn to say no! So many of us feel overwhelmed by life. It feels as if there aren't enough hours in the day to accomplish what we need to. We're tired, we're unmotivated, and we feel a tremendous amount of pressure. It's as if everyone wants or expects something, and satisfying these expectations seems virtually impossible.

Can you relate to any of these feelings? If so, there's no need to worry. Managing your commitments will solve most of these problems, and the first step in doing so is learning to say no. There are only so many hours a day. If you think about it, there are only so many weeks in a month, months in a year, and years in a lifetime. Time is precious, and it's essential to prioritize yours if you want to reach your goals.

How to Say No

Saying no is never easy. Social expectations may vary significantly depending upon what part of the world you live in. If you live in an area that is primarily individualistic, it will be easier say no and do your own thing. If you live in a group-oriented area (such as Japan or other Asian countries), participation in social activities is expected of everyone. That, of course, can make saying no much more challenging.

Regardless of where you reside, the following tips will make it easier to say no:

Be clear on your values and mission in life

It's crucial to know what your values are, what is truly important to you, and what you really want to accomplish. Otherwise, you'll have a harder time prioritizing your activities and saying no to things that aren't in line with your goals. Once you know what you want and what needs to be done to get it, saying no gets much easier.

Learn to express your values

When a friend, colleague, or schoolmate invites you to a social event, are you comfortable declining their invitation? Or do you feel anxious and find yourself mumbling barely intelligible excuses? Or, worse yet, do you tend to say yes even when you don't want to? If the second or third option applies to you, you don't have to feel petrified by the thought of saying no to social invites anymore. Nor do you need to force yourself to socialize when you don't want to.

Instead, take an upfront approach and try to communicate as clearly as you can. Whenever possible, tell the person what you're currently working on and why it means so much to you. If you stay polite yet firm, most people will understand your desire to prioritize that which is dear to you.

Make no apologies for the way you choose to use your time

You don't have to defend the way you spend your time. A lot of people feel pressure to fit in or think that saying no to things is selfish, but that isn't true. It's your life. YOU are the one who gets to choose how best to spend the time you've been granted on this planet. I work in a consulting company of 50 employees. The company's CEO invited me to his place just last week, but I said no. Instead, I worked on my new book about habits. When asked to spend my time on something that isn't in line with my major tasks, I say no whenever I can. Do you?

Learn to care less what people think

It's pretty hard to say no if you're agonizing over what other people think. You'll have to care less about how you're viewed by others and focus more on yourself.

In his book *The Entrepreneur Roller Coaster*, Darren Hardy states that, on average, only 10 people will cry at your funeral. Yes, out of the thousands and thousands of people you meet throughout your life, around 10 will cry at your funeral. Do you know what's even worse? Those who choose not to attend your funeral will do so for a very shocking reason. The main reason most people decide not to attend funerals is...

Wait for it...

The weather!

Yes, the weather. If rain, snow, or other inconvenient weather strikes, some people won't even bother coming.

When you consider things like this, it makes no sense to allow other people to dictate what you do and don't do in your life.

Value yourself and realize that focusing on your priorities will have a positive impact on society

It's important to recognize your worth. Focusing on what truly matters to you will allow you to live a more fulfilling life and positively influence the world around you. So, what's more important, working on something you're passionate about, or going to a cocktail party?

Accept the fact that most people are selfish

 In your 20s and 30s you worry about what people think of you, in your 40s and 50s you stop caring what they think of you. And then, finally, in your 60s and 70s, you realize they were never thinking about you in the first place.

This famous saying speaks volumes.

Yes, most people are too busy thinking about themselves to think about you. So, let's apply this to our earlier discussion of social invitations. When people invite you to something, it's unlikely that they're giving in-depth thought to your happiness, and they probably aren't thinking much about whether you'll genuinely enjoy the outing. For instance, I'm an introvert and to say I'm not fond of parties is an understatement. When a friend invites me to a party, it's usually because they like parties and think it would be fun to have me along. They aren't taking the time to consider whether I'll have fun. There's no malice in this, it all comes back to the fact that most people are too busy tending to their own feelings to figure out what yours are. Only you know what you'll enjoy, so go with your gut.

The point is, you don't owe anyone anything. You should try to spend as much time as possible on what matters to you. You have every right to focus on that which will produce positive changes in your life. In fact, you deserve it.

Real-Life Example:

I avoid committing to things that aren't in line with my ultimate goals whenever possible. If I know that saying yes to something is going to make it harder to achieve what I want and I'm not obligated to do it, I politely decline. Saying no may feel uncomfortable, but training yourself to do it is essential. Here's something to consider the next time you're asked to commit to something: If you could remove all social pressure, would you say yes or no? If you are honest with yourself, you'll already know the answer.

Managing commitments means thinking about what is most important to you. Keep in mind that focusing on what you want and prioritizing your goals is NOT selfish. Are there any extraneous obligations at work, school, or in your personal life that are preventing you from doing this? If so, what can you do about it? Is there something that you always say yes to at the expense of your goals and happiness?

When you first start cutting these things out, some people may be shocked or disappointed. But you can't let that get to you! When you make major changes, those around you often have to adjust to them as much as you do. Fortunately, most people will get used to it and realize that you're just taking your goals seriously. You may even inspire them to do the same!

3

VALUING YOUR TIME

 Money is refundable but time isn't.

— Digyant

One of the biggest lies people tell themselves is that money is not important. Aside from being bullshit, it's a limiting and disempowering belief that will significantly reduce your ability to create wealth. Why, you ask?

Well, for starters, money buys time. That's why increasing your productivity is so important. In doing so you can earn the same amount of money in less time. This will give you free time that you can devote to relaxing, pursuing your passion, or working longer hours if you feel like making even more money.

We can say money is unimportant all we want, but that's a very strange thing to say when we spend most of our time at work trying to make ends meet. If money isn't important, then why are you willing to spend 40-plus years of your life working at a job you have little interest in or maybe even hate? You're doing it to make money, right? See how flawed this way of thinking is and how harmful it can be? If you'd like more information on dangerous beliefs that can hold you back, check out my article « [4 Disempowering Beliefs That Keep You Poor](#) » on my blog.

At this point, you might be thinking, "Okay, money is absolutely essential…so how could time be more important than money?"

The answer is relatively simple. By using the information within this book to increase your levels of productivity, you can find many ways to generate more money. You can't, however, generate more time. Time is a depreciating asset. It decreases every second and there is absolutely nothing we can do about it.

This brings me to my next point: Don't use your time to save money, but rather, use your money to save time.

We all know that time is not infinite, yet many people act as if they'll live forever. Most people spend their time searching for ways to save money when they should be looking for ways to make more of it. They spend hours looking for coupons online just to save a few bucks at the local supermarket. Or they'll waste time going to a certain store just because there's a limited-time discount, only to wait in line with other people who also enjoy wasting their time.

It's no accident that wealthy people understand how precious their time is. If you earned $100 or more per hour would you spend an hour looking for coupons to save a few bucks? You wouldn't, unless coupon-hunting is actually fun for you.

Wealthy people understand how valuable their time is, but do you? Learning to value your time will automatically increase your ability to become more productive. But you can't increase the level to which you value your time until you find out how much you value it to begin with. Sadly, most of us undervalue our time, and this tendency often stems from undervaluing ourselves.

To find out how much one hour of your time is worth, you have to be clear on what you'd like to earn each month. I'll give you a formula that will help you figure this stuff out, but I need you to consider your hourly wage first. And when I say hourly wage, I mean what you earn after factoring in the time and money you put into performing your job. How much time do you spend commuting? How much do you spend on gas, bus passes, or subway tickets? These are just two of several factors to take into account. For clarity's sake, let's refer to the number you arrive at as your Adjusted Monthly Salary. Divide it by the number of hours you spend at work or performing work-related tasks and voila! There's your true hourly wage. It's lower than you realized, right?

Unfortunately, many people who analyze their hourly wage this way will realize that it's not that high. And remember, we aren't even considering what you spend on work clothes, shoes, or rent (some people have to live in an area that's more expensive than they'd like so that they can be closer to their job). And we certainly haven't factored in how physically and emotionally draining your job might be.

Yet this doesn't have to be a depressing discovery. In fact, it can open you up to new possibilities. If your job is unreasonably draining and you're putting a lot of money towards work-related expenses that aren't covered by your company, discovering your hourly wage is lower than you'd like might be the push you need to consider finding a new job. You can look for something that pays more or offers more hours. Keep in mind, however, that this may not fully resolve your problems.

In Japan, where I've been living for 8 years, it's not rare for people to work 60 to 70 hours per week just to earn an *average* salary. You might think that a 60 to 70-hour workweek should result in decent money, but that's not necessarily true. When you add the time and stress involved in commuting, other work-related tasks and obligations, and the cost of living in a big city like Tokyo, the hourly wage *still* comes up pretty low!

Higher-paying jobs still require out-of-pocket work expenses, and landing a job that requires even more hours than your previous one is probably less than appealing. Fortunately, there are still other options. How about starting a home-based business? It may sound fantastical, but you'd be surprised at how many people have online businesses or do freelance work from the comfort of a home-office. And, surprisingly enough, some companies actually have work-from-home positions.

Any of these options would allow you to decrease work-related expenses, reduce stress levels, and improve your overall well-being. You wouldn't be tied to a specific location, so you could even move to a cheaper city.

Achieving these things probably sounds difficult, but it might be easier than it seems. More importantly, working online enables you to work on earning passive income, which makes it much easier to achieve your ideal income.

Steve Pavlina has a fantastic article on the differences between a traditional jobs and those that generate passive income. I strongly suggest you give it a read! It's pretty entertaining.

The Real Cost of Undervaluing Yourself

Devaluing your time can significantly reduce your earning potential. People who don't value their time tend to sell their products and services for far less than what they are worth. This often repels would-be clients or customers because, believe it or not, things that are set at unreasonably low prices come off as cheap and not worth buying. Needless to say, selling your products or services for too little is harmful on multiple levels. It decreases your earnings, diminishes your productivity, and blocks would-be clients from the benefits of your product.

Once again, understanding how much your time is truly work is crucial to increasing your productivity. That's where the Dan Lok's method, referred to as the F.U. Money calculator, comes in. Remember that formula I said I'd show you earlier? This is it! This calculator will give you an idea of the hourly wage necessary to reach your ideal income. Here's how it works:

Define your target, or rather, how much money you'd like to earn each month. For example's sake, let's say that you want to earn $10,000 a month.

Plug in the number of hours you work per month (let's say 150), and assume that you're productive for only half of those hours. Dan Lok says that just one-third of our work hours are actually productive, but I'll be generous with you.

Plug these numbers into the following formula: The Amount of Money You Wish to Earn/ (The Amount of Hours You work/2) = How Your Time is Worth. When using the numbers in the numbers in the example, the formula would look like this: 10,000/(150h/2) = $133. This would mean that your time is worth $133 per hour.

And there you have it! That's how much your time is worth. Of course, it may take a while before you're earning the amount of money necessary to reach your financial target. That's okay, however, because simply reminding yourself of how much your time is worth will allow you to value your time (and yourself!) more. As a result, you'll always be looking for ways to heighten your productivity and increase your hourly wage. If you're earning $30 per hour but know you need an hourly wage of $133 to reach your monthly target of $10,000, your outlook will change. You'll spend more time on your most productive tasks and will try to increase your efficiency by delegating or outsourcing any tasks that aren't worth $133 per hour.

So now it's up to you. What can you do *right now* to increase your productivity per hour?

4

THINKING DIFFERENTLY

 We cannot solve our problems with the same thinking we used when we created them.

— ALBERT EINSTEIN

When it comes to making lasting changes in our lives, changing the way we think is among the most important factors. It's difficult to get out of a rut when you're thinking the same way you did when you got into it. If your mind is closed to certain possibilities, then you'll miss out on a wide variety of opportunities.

When attempting to combat this common problem, it's crucial to make a habit of stepping back and considering the big picture. It's easy to miss the many ways we can become more efficient, streamline our approaches, and minimize time-wasting. Big goals may be easier to manage when you take them step by step or day by day. However, it's possible to focus too narrowly and become so consumed with day-to-day activities that you sabotage your long-term goals.

It's advisable to use the Maverick Paradigm, The Lazy Man Paradigm, and The Busy Man Paradigm to help you spot time-wasters, areas of inefficiency, and missed opportunities.

The Maverick Paradigm

To utilize the Maverick Paradigm, ask yourself if there are areas in which you could or should do things differently. Are there just a few areas, or do you need to change your approach in its entirety? Are there things that you're spending time on that, upon further examination, seem unnecessary?

Sometimes we get so used to doing the same thing over and over again that we don't notice new ways to improve our productivity. This is one of the reasons big companies hire consultants so frequently. Consultants are exposed to a lot of different industries and can often take ideas and technologies from other industries and apply them to their client's company. The client, however, can't see beyond their own industry, which they have spent many years working in. More often than not, the client has developed an unconscious tendency to do things the way they've always been done, and it takes a consultant to halt the stagnation.

Now it's your turn! Are there things you could do differently at work or in your personal life to amplify your productivity and free up your time? If you're not quite sure about what you can change, the following questions will help:

- What would you do if you were the CEO of your company?
- What would you do if you had only one year to double the company's revenue?
- What would your friends or relatives do if they were in your shoes and wanted to become more productive?

The Lazy Man Paradigm

The Lazy Man Paradigm might seem counterintuitive. But a lot can happen when you look at things from a lazy perspective while keeping your goals and objectives in mind. You can, in fact, discover new ways of doing things. In some cases, you can drastically increase your productivity. You might not come up with any good ideas at first. But, by continuously training your brain to adopt this paradigm, you'll build a mindset that allows you to achieve what you want with fewer resources, whether those resources are time, energy, money, or something else.

To implement the Lazy Man Paradigm, you should start by asking yourself the following questions: What would I do if I were the laziest person in the world? What would I cut back on? What would I view as extraneous? Then, ask yourself if the things you would cut back can be eliminated, outsourced or delegated (more on this in the next chapter!). Finally, assess whether the things you find extraneous have any legitimate necessity.

Consider the following questions:

- If I were allowed to completely remove certain tasks from my job, what would they be?
- What tasks can I outsource or delegate?
- What tasks am I terrible at? What task can almost everyone else do better than me?
- Can I work 2 hours less per week? How about 5 or 10?
- Can I work 4 days per week instead of 5? How about 3?

Real-Life Example

I work in consulting, and my job often requires me to find specific information for my clients. I devote a significant amount of time to research, and used to start certain things from scratch when I didn't need to. This led to lots of stress, and there were times when I was burning the candle at both ends to complete my tasks.

Though it's not always possible to streamline my research, I've now trained myself to look for ways to get things done with as little effort as possible. Instead of delving immediately into research, I try to see if there is anyone who already has some, if not all, of the information I need. When I find such a person, it saves me a lot of time. I also consider whether my company could outsource some of the research and use that extra time to develop strategies to better serve our customers. Last but not least, I reuse templates and documents whenever possible, and only create new ones when I know that none of the preexistent ones will work.

The Busy Man Paradigm

 If you want something done, ask a busy person to do it. The more things you do, the more you can do.

— Lucille Ball

The Busy Man Paradigm is, like the other two paradigms mentioned, relatively simple. While the Maverick Paradigm helps you discover new ways of increasing your productivity and the Lazy Man Paradigm conserves resources, the Busy Man Paradigm helps you clarify your priorities. As Parkinson's Law states, "Work expands so as to fill in the time available for its completion."

Now, take a look at the tasks and goals that you're trying to accomplish, and then imagine having only a month to accomplish them. What about a week? How about a day? Consider what could be done in those timeframes, and what you would do to find a way to complete everything within each of those timeframes

The things you come up with will tell you what you should be thinking about and focusing on in regards to getting things accomplished. As I've said before, it's easy to give into fear and put off what we know we should be doing. Spending hours reading books and watching YouTube tutorials might sound like a good idea, and you can certainly learn from them. But who do you think is being more productive: the guy who spends 7 hours a day taking action and only 1 hour reading, or the guy who spends 7 hours reading and just 1 taking action? I know from experience. I used to be the first guy, but I'm now more like the second.

If you were the busiest man in the world, what tasks would you concentrate on? How much time would you really need to accomplish these tasks?

5
PRIORITIZING EFFICIENTLY

 Lack of time is actually lack of priorities.

— Tim Ferris

Prioritizing involves figuring out what is most important and consistently putting it first. Most people have a lot going on in their lives and feel overwhelmed. They haven't found the time to reevaluate their lives, clarify what their goals are, and see if what they're devoting their time to is truly worthwhile. Lacking priorities is usually a sign that your sense of direction isn't clear enough. This leads to a sense of confusion and makes it easy to take on too many things at once.

When this happens, there's a huge risk of neglecting what really matters and feeling that, as busy as you are, you should be accomplishing more and getting better results. This is where another often overlooked aspect of prioritizing comes in: weeding out low-priority activities and tasks. The key to efficient prioritizing is doing less to give yourself more time to focus on things that are essential to your success.

For optimal prioritizing, it's crucial to focus on the following activities: delegating, outsourcing, postponing, and removing.

Delegating/Outsourcing

Delegating and outsourcing are a good idea when you find that there are low-value tasks that can be done more effectively (and ideally at a lower cost) by someone else. There are a wide range of things that can be delegated or outsourced, such as basic research and repetitive tasks.

Eventually, anything for which the cost per hour is less than your hourly wage should be outsourced. As Darren Hardy mentioned in his book *The Entrepreneur RollerCoaster* "You need to be constantly asking yourself, "Would I pay someone (the hourly rate we just determined above) to do what I'm doing now?".

Using freelance websites is one of the easiest ways to start delegating. It's possible to find good freelancers who charge very little simply because the cost of living is far lower in their country than it is in yours.

Real-Life Example:

If I tried to create my book covers myself, it would take me LOT of time. Because designing isn't one of my skills, it's unlikely I'd have finished it in time. I would have been spending tons of time on something without even getting the results I wanted. And that is why I chose to outsource the cover design.

By doing this, the cover was completed much faster than I could have done it and the quality was far better than anything I could've achieved on my own. And, because it cost much less than what an hour of my time is valued at, it saved money. While there are multiple websites that can connect you to high-quality freelancers, I use UpWork and Fiverr.

Outsourcing in Your Personal Life

Work and projects aren't the only things that can be outsourced or delegated, however. Our personal lives are often rife with tasks and obligations that, while necessary, take up a lot of our time without doing much to bring us closer to our goals. Cooking, cleaning, gardening, and running errands are prime examples of this. While it's impractical to assign all of these things to other people, and many of us wouldn't want to even if we could, you probably feel that at least one of these tasks would be better left to someone else.

Start by asking yourself what among your current tasks drives you crazy, and what you aren't particularly good at. Do you cringe at the thought of picking weeds and mowing grass? Does going to the grocery store feel like a hassle? Are you the kind of person who burns grilled cheese and can't seem to get their popcorn right? Do you put off cleaning your home because you can't find the time? If there's something you can't stand doing, don't have the time for, or just can't seem to do well, you may want to consider delegating or outsourcing it.

Real-Life Example 1:

I loathe cleaning my apartment, so I've been considering hiring someone to do it. Yes, it's an expenditure, but if I take the time I would normally spend cleaning and put it into writing more books and producing more content for my website, I'll be happier and more productive. I'll also generate more money than what I would pay for an hour of professional cleaning services. Last but not least, the person I hire will likely clean faster and better than I do.

Real-Life Example 2:

I have a friend whose sister dislikes going to the grocery store. She knows it's necessary and feels that it shouldn't be a big deal, but the nearest grocery store isn't all that close. Standing in lines, going through the aisles, and spending time just standing there trying to find the best prices irritate her and make her feel like she's wasting her time. She doesn't like wasting the gas, either. She solved this problem by shopping at a grocery chain that offered a delivery service. This allowed her to quickly compile a list, remove items that she found at a better price and switch them for their cheaper counterparts, and simply wait for the items to arrive. Although there is a small delivery fee, she finds more bargains when she shops online (perhaps because she's not irritated and in a rush). Better still, the delivery fee winds up being less than what she spends on gas to get to the store. She now uses the time she once spent at the grocery store to use her home gym, which directly supports her weight-loss goals.

Delegating things You aren't good At

We can't be good at everything, and it would make us miserable to try. When it comes to your success, knowing your weak points is as important as knowing your strengths. You'll never become a highly productive person if you don't learn to focus only on the few things you do extremely well. When you find yourself facing repetitive tasks or tasks that are not your forte, you should, whenever possible, delegate them to someone who can do them well.

Unfortunately, few people know how to delegate effectively, and many people find it too costly. Are you unwilling to delegate things you aren't good at or don't enjoy doing because you think it is "too expensive"? If so, you probably aren't valuing yourself and your time as much as you should.

Productive people often have an assistant, a cook, a housekeeper, or someone else that helps them in a certain area. They also tend to utilize delivery services and things that streamline their lives. This isn't because they are lazy, (they are usually hard workers), it's because understand how valuable their time is. If you earned $500 per hour would you spend an entire afternoon mowing the lawn? If you like it, then maybe. If you don't, then probably not!

You might argue that it's easy to for people to delegate when they've got plenty of money available for that. However, part of the reason they make so much money is because they delegate minor tasks. Doing so gives them more time to focus on things that provide fulfillment and generate money. So, what may seem like an expenditure can quickly become an integral part of increasing your income.

Real-Life Example 1:

As a native of France, I'm not that good at writing in English, at least when it comes to the amount of writing necessary for a book. On top of that, my job doesn't allow me much free time. Rather than pushing myself to write this entire book myself and sacrificing time and quality in the process, I hired a native English speaker to help me write parts of the book. This allowed me to focus on creating the outline and optimizing the content while delegating less important parts like specific examples.

This sped up the process significantly, and allowed me to produce an easy-to-read book with high-quality English.

It also gave me the opportunity to maximize the value of the book's content by utilizing my preexistent knowledge and previous experiences. By delegating some of the writing to someone with stronger skills, I was able to maintain high-quality without sacrificing productivity. As with most forms of delegation or outsourcing, it wasn't free. However, it takes more time and money to write a book whose English will need to be heavily edited than it does to hire a good freelancer to help you write a high-quality book.

Real-Life Example 2:

I know someone who purchased a home with a lush but high-maintenance backyard and a garden that was difficult to sustain. He wasn't particularly good at yardwork, nor did he do well with plants. Sometimes keeping up the yard and garden even made him sick by worsening his seasonal allergies. His long work hours made it difficult to find the time to eat regularly, let alone tend to the backyard. After several months of frustration, dead plants, overgrown foliage, and even a note from the Homeowner's Association, he ultimately decided to hire a gardener to come by every so often. In addition to offering obvious benefits such as more time, a nice-looking backyard, and decreased stress, it also made him healthier. His allergy attacks decreased, he had more energy, and was able to spend more time on taking care of himself and doing things that he enjoyed. Most importantly, he figured out a way to handle an overwhelming task that could be helpful in other areas of life.

Postponing Tasks

The word 'postpone', along with its synonym delay, holds a negative connotation for many people. This isn't surprising, considering the fact that procrastination, one of the enemies of productivity, involves putting things off to another time. However, there is a big difference between postponement and procrastination. While procrastination entails dragging your feet on important tasks and delaying the pursuit of your goals in favor of busywork, postponement is limited to minor tasks or tasks unrelated to your current major goal. When it comes to things that are low on your list of priorities, postponement can be a good thing. I'll go into further detail about this in the chapter on focus.

Real-Life Example 1:

There are so many things I wish I could do simultaneously. If I had infinite time, I would be training to become a life-coach, studying to be a hypnotherapist, getting into public speaking, learning more about copywriting, and exploring the world of online marketing etc. However, with a full time job (and even without), it's unrealistic to pursue so many things at once.

You'll get much further by focusing on one thing for a while and postponing other activities in the meantime. Being obsessed with one thing is generally more effective than perpetual multi-tasking. In fact, one of the main reasons people fail is because they suffer from "Shiny Object Syndrome". They jump from one goal to another and hop from one opportunity to the next in an attempt to accomplish everything at once. But in the end, they realize they haven't accomplished much. Does it sound familiar? I can definitely relate to it myself. Postponing is learning to say "no" now, but "maybe" in the future when your priorities change.

Removal is yet another facet of prioritizing, and it is sometimes a precursor to implementing the first two (delegating and outsourcing). Sometimes, no matter how much you delegate or outsource, you will still find yourself overwhelmed, with barely enough time and energy to attend to the basics, let alone take consistent daily steps towards your goals. When this happens, it's usually a sign that you need to eliminate unnecessary tasks, activities, or even relationships.

Delegation and outsourcing work best after all unnecessary work has been eliminated. As always, it's important to keep your specific goals in mind when determining what you need to remove or take a break from in your life. After considering your main objectives, ask yourself if there is anything you're giving your energy to that does not positively impact your ability to reach your goals. Unless this thing is necessary for you to cover life's basic necessities, it might be time to stop doing it.

Real-Life Example 2

Let's say your schedule is jam-packed with social events, volunteer work, or hobbies. Perhaps you go to the movies with a friend every Friday, or you're taking classes in something that you enjoy but isn't unrelated to your goals. Maybe you spend several hours a week volunteering somewhere, or you work out on a daily basis. Or perhaps you tend to marathon T.V. shows to unwind.

You don't necessarily have to eliminate all of these activities. For the most part, they're harmless and even healthy (in moderation, of course). But if you don't have time to pursue your goals, you would definitely need to cut back on them. Do you really need to go to the movies every Friday? What if you did it twice a month instead? Can you take a break from your classes until you're further along in your goal or have more free time? How about shaving an hour or two off of your volunteer work? Would cutting out a couple of workouts each week cause any real problems? And is it possible to replace television binges with something that doesn't soak up so much time? Some of these activities could be completely eliminated without any adverse effects, and virtually all of them could be scaled down.

Richard Branson: An Example of Extreme Focus

A company wanted to hire Richard Branson, the billionaire founder of Virgin, as a keynote speaker. They first offered him $100,000 for an hour-long speech, but he declined. They raised their offer to $250,000, but again he declined. Then $500,000, but still no. Finally, they offered to pay whatever price he named. Despite this lucrative offer, they received the following message from his office:

No amount of money would matter. Right now, Richard has three strategic priorities he is focused on, and he will only allow us to allocate his calendar to something that significantly contributes to the accomplishment of one of those three priorities, and speaking for a fee is not one of them.

What about you? What activities can you remove in your life?

Firing your customers

If you're in business, firing some of your customers might be another necessity. Many of us have been taught that the customer is always right, and that our success is completely dependent upon the number of clients we have. It's important to provide your customers with good service and a pleasant experience, and they are an important part of your business. But remember the 80/20 rule, which is based on the following statistic: 80% of your revenue comes from a mere 20% of your customers. This means that, if necessary, you can thin out your client base without hurting your business.

In fact, the increased productivity will probably have a positive influence on it. This is even more true when it comes to problem customers. If you have customers who, despite your best efforts, are never satisfied, complain constantly, and are always stressing you out, it's best to drop them. Unhealthy business relationships are a drain on energy and resources, and it's better to take the time you save by eliminating unreasonable customers and devote it to your loyal customers with whom you have healthy business relationships.

Real-Life Example:

For health reasons, my father was forced to reduce the number of hours he worked each week. This seemed like a bad thing at first, as working less generally means earning less. Yet, he found himself earning more than he did before cutting back on his hours. He reduced his workload by cutting ties with problem customers and focused his efforts on maintaining good clients. Decreasing the quantity of your work may seem counterintuitive, but, as long as you maintain or increase the quality, it can be a wonderful thing. You even may find yourself experiencing an increase in referral-based revenue and an enhanced ability to get things done, both of which fuel a healthy business.

6
FOCUSING

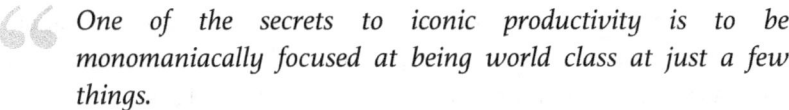 *One of the secrets to iconic productivity is to be monomaniacally focused at being world class at just a few things.*

— Robin Sharma

When asked about the most important factors in their success, both Bill Gates and Warren Buffet gave the same answer: Focus.

In a book co-written with Buffet, author Alice Schroeder elaborated on this by saying that focus was key for him and that he, "...ruled out paying attention to almost anything but business—art, literature, science, travel, architecture—so that he could focus on his passion."

His focus extended to the way he managed his employees. He would ask them to come up with 25 tasks to work on, and then circle only 5 of them. He would then tell them to focus *exclusively* on these 5 tasks. To him, what remained was more than just low-priority tasks. They were distractions that needed to be avoided at all costs! They were dangerous threats to success. Productivity is not just what you do, it's also what you choose *not* to do.

I can certainly relate to this in my life. There are so many things that have the potential to distract us. It's easy to think, "Let me just watch this one video, it might help", "I'll just try out this small business idea on the side", or "I'm only going to read one more book." However, I've trained myself to focus on one thing until I get the results I want. After that, I may or may not venture in other businesses or tackle other major goals that I have in life. What about you? Have you experienced the same problem?

As you can see, trying to do too much at once is one of the most common traps when it comes to staying focused and productive. Almost all of us have something we want to change in our lives, and most us have several somethings that we'd like to change. It's tempting to try making all of these changes simultaneously or in quick succession, but this rarely turns out the way we want it to.

Many of us start out the New Year with plenty of resolutions and the motivation and determination to go with them. We want to lose weight, exercise more, earn a promotion, calm our minds, learn a new language, become more well read...the list goes on and on. At first, we make progress. We get slimmer, become more active, work longer hours, eat better, and meditate. We read new books, pick up new hobbies, and whatever engage in whatever other activities support our new goals. This can't be sustained indefinitely, however, and it isn't long before we're worn out. The next thing we know, we're burnt out and can't continue any longer. When this happens, most of us become discouraged and give up. We think we've failed and can't reach our goals when, in reality, we simply neglected to pace ourselves.

If this is something you've experienced before, it doesn't have to happen again. Think back on the progress you made before burning out. Imagine if you focused on just one of the goals you set out to accomplish and tackled them one by one? What do you think you could've accomplished if you'd stuck with that one goal as long as you planned? Probably a lot, right? Well, why not look back on your list of goals and choose one that you still feel passionately about, the one that will have the most impact in your life? If you focus exclusively on that goal, you'll wind up accomplishing more than you thought possible.

If you have more than one goal you'd like to achieve, tackle them one-by-one. Focus on the goal that will make the biggest difference in your life. When you concentrate on one thing at a time, you're able to give your all to whatever you're focusing on. This leads to faster results and an increased likelihood that you'll reach your goal. Furthermore, the accomplishment of one goal will provide momentum that can fuel the pursuit of your next goal.

Also, when you are perfectly clear on what your goal is, it becomes easier to avoid distractions and say no to anything that isn't closely related to your goal. You just have to ask yourself each time: "is this activity helping me achieve my goals?"

The next time you find yourself tempted to pursue a wide range of goals at once, consider the fact that your motivation and willpower will eventually dip. Remember that pursuing multiple goals will become tiresome. Instead, choose one area of your life (such as personal growth, career, finances, or relationships), and spend the majority of your time and effort making the changes you'd like to see.

So, what is your one goal?

The Power of a Singular Focus

> *I fear not the man who has practiced 10,000 kicks once, but I fear the man who has practiced one kick 10,000 times.*
>
> — Bruce Lee

As previously stated, choosing to focus on just one thing can work wonders when it comes to reaching your goals. However, choosing one thing when there are many things you want to accomplish can be difficult. In *The ONE Thing,* a powerful book that details the benefits of narrowing your focus to a single thing, the reader is asked the following question: What's the ONE Thing you can do such that by doing it everything else will be easier or unnecessary? Your answer to this question is invaluable.

Real-Life Example 1:

An example of what you can do when you adopt a singular focus can be found in the following excerpt from *The ONE Thing*

> ...As fast as we were growing, we were still not acknowledged by the top people in our industry. I challenged our group to brainstorm 100 ways to turn this situation around. It took us all day to come up with the list. The next morning, we narrowed the list down to ten ideas, and from there we chose just one big idea. The one that we decided on was that I would write a book on how to become an elite performer in our industry. It worked. Eight years later that one book had not only become a national bestseller, but also had morphed into a series of books with total sales of over a million copies. In an industry of about a million people, one thing changed our image forever.

Real-Life Example 2:

I asked myself plenty of questions when contemplating what my 'one thing' was, but the most important one was this: What is the one thing that I can do to generate passive income in such a way that doing it will make everything else easier or unnecessary?

I thought of multiple things, but my best answer was this: Focus on writing books and generating passive income. I could have decided to spend time working on my blog and writing guest posts on other blogs. I could have started the process of becoming a Certified Life Coach and Hypnotherapist, among other things. Now, these are all things that I will do in the future. But with a job that requires 50 to 60 hours of my week, it is not currently feasible. More importantly, focusing on these things won't bring me any real results in the near future. As such, there's only one thing I ask myself: What did I do today that will help me generate passive income in the near future?

7

USING THE POWER OF LEVERAGE

 Leverage is maximum productivity with minimum effort.

— Dan Lok

Leverage involves using what you have to its maximum potential. When you leverage your resources, you take full advantage of what's at your disposal. The following 5 things are particularly useful sources of leverage: audience, content, technology, resources, and money. Now that you know what some of the best sources of leverage are, let's talk about how to use them.

Leveraging Your Audience

In regards to an audience, the more people that can benefit from your work, the more money you're likely to earn. This, in turn, means higher levels of productivity per hour.

Real-Life Example:

Let's just say that you're giving an hour-long speech to a group of 100 people, each of whom is willing to pay $5 for your speech. That gives you $500. Of course, you must also consider the amount of time required the prepare the speech as well as money you put into renting the room, promoting the event, and other such things. Still, $500 isn't bad, and if your audience doubles, suddenly you have $1,000. As you can see, the amount of money that you earn can increase drastically based on the number of people that find value in your work. And, it doesn't require than you work harder.

Leveraging Content

Leveraging content involves utilizing what you have already created to reach more people or expand and create even more content.

Real-Life Example:

Suppose you've done the same speech more than 20 times. At that point, you probably won't have to spend much time preparing it, so your overall productivity will increase. You'll earn the same amount of money you did when you first started giving the speech, if not more, all while decreasing the amount of time and effort it takes to do so.

As such, you're technically earning more money per hour, and can use the time you no longer have to spend on your speech and put it towards something else that gets you closer to your goals.

Additionally, you can write a book or produce other written content based upon some of the concepts in your speech. This will allow you to make the most of what you create and will also make it easier to reach a wider audience.

Or perhaps you can create a series of short books based upon a portion of your book that you'd like to cover in further detail. It's always possible to discuss a topic from your previous work in more detail, and elaborating on more complex topics will generate further content.

This, of course, is likely to attract people who are already purchasing your work and want more of it. There may be people who had too much general knowledge of the topic of your first book to see value in it, but who are willing to purchase the new content to get detailed information on the subject. There are infinite ways to reach a wider audience!

To give you a concrete example, I sometimes reuse some of the content of my blog in my books, and vice-versa. In the future, I may also use some of the content in my books and blog to create a course.

Reusing the content you've already produced is (usually) not a bad thing. It allows you to reach out to a broader audience by leveraging different medias (books, videos, one-one-one interaction, seminars etc.) Also, by presenting information in a different way you may reach people who didn't connect with your previous work but find your new product, service, or method of delivery valuable.

Finally, it's important to understand the importance of repetition when it comes to personal development. As is the case with many other subjects, people often need to be exposed to an idea multiple before they fully understand its value. Jim Rohn, one of my favorite personal development figures, had a story that he would repeat at each and every one of his seminars. When asked why he always told the same story over and over, he replied that he would tell it again and again until people got it.

I can attest to this, as it took me a long time to fully understand basic concepts (such as the power of focusing on just a few things at a time).

The bottom line is this: reusing the content you already have is often beneficial, and you shouldn't be afraid to do so.

Leveraging Technology

Leveraging technology is connected with utilizing the first two sources of leverage: content and audience. The ability to create websites, use social media platforms, and make use of video hosting sites makes leveraging technology easier than ever.

Real-Life Example:

By harnessing technology in all its forms, you can go beyond using the concepts in your speech to create and sell books on the internet. You can actually use some of the content from your books to create articles. You can then post these articles on your website or blog as a means of promotion. You can also post your articles to other websites, and with a little networking you can write some guests posts on someone else's blog. While you're at it, you can make videos based on the content of your books and speeches.

You can even create some sort of course that helps your readers implement the information that is in your books. Whether it's a video course, a written course, or a combination of both, you can market it alongside your book.

You can do any of these things, or even all of them, and that's just the tip of the iceberg. The possibilities are endless. The internet is teeming with ways to broaden your reach and promote your work. Your creativity is the only limit!

The use of technology can do more than just broaden your audience, however. It can also help streamline the process of content creation, thus increasing productivity and enabling you to make more money with less effort.

What about you? Is there a way you can leverage technology to enhance your productivity and increase the quality of your work?

Leveraging Resources

Outsourcing is the first step to leveraging your resources. As I mentioned earlier, outsourcing involves the following 2 things:

Identifying tasks that are overwhelming, beyond your skill set, or otherwise unpalatable.

Assigning those tasks to someone who can do them better, faster, and (hopefully) cheaper than you.

Real-Life Example:

Let's assume you have a business that offers an array of cool products. You'd have to devote a lot of time to the creation, design, and distribution of your products, to say nothing of promotional work. There would also be a host of necessary activities that are of rather low value (think research and other repetitive tasks).

You could attempt to do everything yourself or within your company, but you'd end up wasting a lot of time, which would probably diminish the quality of your products. Wouldn't it be better to hire some freelancers to handle these tasks?

Outsourcing low value tasks enables you to focus on more important things. Why not hire a virtual assistant, freelance writer, or data entry specialist to help with promotional work, bookkeeping, or product descriptions?

Many freelancers actually specialize in these tasks. Utilizing their expertise will allow you to concentrate on improving the quality of your current products while creating some awesome new ones.

In what way could you use outsourcing to improve the quality of your business, products, or content?

Leveraging Money

It's easier to go where the money is, and leveraging money means considering your target audience. It's advisable to set your sights on audiences that might be willing and able to pay more for your content than others. By doing this, you can increase your income without any extra work.

Real-Life Example:

There are multiple audiences that you could address a speech to. You could easily give a speech to high-school students, retired workers, or the employees of a small business. But what if you could address a speech to the employees of a multibillion-dollar company? For a company of that size, paying you $5,000 to $10,000 for your time probably won't be as big a deal as it would be for groups with smaller budgets.

This might mean you have to spend a bit of time making minor adjustments so that the content of your speech is tailored to the higher-paying group. However, this is a small investment and the return is well worth it.

An additional benefit of playing to a higher-paying crowd is that it increases the amount of value others associate with your skill, service, or product. When people are aware that there are others who are willing to pay a good price for what you have to offer, they are likely to see it as being worth more than they would if you were catering to lower-paying groups.

Furthermore, when you do end up offering your services to those who pay less, they may feel as though they are getting your products, knowledge, or services at a discount. When comparing their payment to that of higher-paying groups, they'll feel like they're getting something special.

This may make them more eager to book you, because it will be as if your work is on sale. Sales don't last forever, and they will probably feel the need to strike while the iron is hot. They'll be anxious to book you before you get a chance to strike a deal with a higher-paying group instead. This creates an increased sense of demand for your service, content, or products that can give you more opportunities to grow your audience and reach more people.

These are just some of many examples, but they provide an overview of the multitude of things you can do when you utilize the power of leverage. Now, it's your turn! Take some time to think of some of the other possibilities. How can you use leverage in your life to increase your productivity?

8

CREATING AN ENVIRONMENT THAT SUPPORTS PRODUCTIVITY

 You are the average of the five people you spend the most time with.

— JIM ROHN

Creating an environment that supports your efforts to reach your goals is another important part of productivity. Willpower doesn't last forever, so you need to have something that makes completing your tasks and projects as easy as possible. You need to be in an environment that will fuel and motivate you long after your willpower is gone. Note that this portion of the book will tackle general goals and large projects rather than daily tasks. Those will resurface again later.

Stick to One Role Model

There are several ways you can create an environment that's conducive to your reaching your goals. For starters, it's important to have a role model. That said, it's best to choose one and stick with them. Having multiple role models for each area of your life that you'd like to improve will leave you scattered and confused. You'll be jumping from one person to another, one blog to the next, and chasing seminar after seminar. Don't become a seminar junkie! Last but not least, keep in mind that your role model can be anyone, whether it's a friend, co-worker, relative, or blogger.

If you find it hard to choose one role model, don't worry. Just think about all of your role models and ask yourself these two questions: Who do you trust most? Who, if you were to consistently act upon their advice, would create the biggest changes in your life?

Stick to One Area at a Time

Resist the temptation of trying to change multiple areas of your life at the same time, because you'll end up failing at all of them. What area of your life would have the most impact on your happiness and productivity? Pick one and focus on it until you see the results that you want.

Focus on One Major Task

What's one thing in the area you selected that would bring results if done consistently? Maybe it's learning and mastering a skill that would significantly improve your productivity at work. Maybe it's walking for an hour every day. Or perhaps it's writing for 90 minutes every morning.

Maintaining a singular focus significantly increases your chances of success, and the 1 x 1 x 1 Rule can help you sustain it. It's relatively simple and, at this point, you've already put some thought into the questions it begs. To implement this rule, choose one area of your life that you'd like to change, what task you'd like to focus on, and one role model to look to. Once you've got that down, you can use the 1 x 1 x 1 Rule to make major changes in your life.

The 90 x 90 x1 Rule works well with the 1 x 1 x 1 Rule. Created by Robin Sharma, this rule requires that you spend the first 90 minutes of your day focusing on your most important tasks for a 90-day period. For the 30-Day Challenge I recommend spending between 60 to 90 minutes on your tasks.

The Power of Accountability

Accountability is crucial to staying productive and is an important part of nurturing your personal growth. One of the best ways to encourage accountability is, as you may have guessed, having an accountability partner. This is someone who understands you, knows your goals, and will hold you to the promises you make to yourself.

A mastermind group provides the support of an accountability partner, but in higher concentrations. Such a group should consist of others who are trying to make big changes in their lives, preferably changes that are similar to yours.

As with accountability partners, it's important for members of your mastermind group to be encouraging people with positive attitudes. Together, you can support one another, help each other overcome obstacles, and provide external motivation to continue working towards your goals.

Success, Failure, and the Company You Keep

If you want to succeed, you must be extremely mindful of who you spend your time with. I can't stress that enough. Your friends are a huge part of your life, and I can guarantee they will influence it far more than you think. As Jim Rohn says, you're the average of the five people you spend the most time with. In other words, you're only as good as the company you keep. When it comes to achieving your goals, few things are as important as your ability to create a positive environment for yourself.

No matter how driven and independent you are, being surrounded by negative, underachieving people who don't support you will lead you to failure. Avoid them like the plague! Always seek out people who are more successful than you. These people will raise your standards, inspire you to achieve more, and, as a by-product, increase your productivity, too! So, again, surround yourself with successful people who have done or are doing what you're trying to do. Neglecting to do so can mean the difference between success and failure.

Are you currently surrounded by extremely productive people? If not, what can you do to change this?

9

PLANNING

 Failing to plan is planning to fail.

— Alan Lakein

Behind every great achievement is an equally great plan. In the words of Robin Sharma, the things that get scheduled are the things that get done. Scheduling your activities is a must. The more specific your plans are, the more productive you will be. Make a habit of planning your month the day before it starts, planning your week every Sunday morning, and planning for tomorrow before you go to bed.

I always accomplish a lot more when I plan than I do when I don't. According to Brian Tracy, one of the world's top goal-setting experts, each minute you spend in planning saves 10 minutes in execution. Simply put, time spent planning means less time spent doing. Planning helps you reach your goals more quickly and efficiently.

Why You Should Plan your Day

The reasons you should plan your day are endless, but let's take a look at the top 7:

1) **It will be easier to avoid distractions.** When you know exactly what you need to do, it's harder for your brain to come up with excuses or reasons to procrastinate. Whenever you put yourself in a situation where you have to think about what to do next, you give your brain an opportunity to look for distractions. You might feel the sudden urge to check your emails, go on Facebook, or watch videos on YouTube. If you're not careful, you can easily waste hours of your time on these things. *Be aware of the fact that your mind will almost always try to distract you, and be on the lookout for the ways in which this manifests.* Feel free to reread the section on procrastination if you need to.

2) **Planning enables you to reflect on your strategy.** It gives you an opportunity to step back and look at the bigger picture. You can assess the efficiency of what you're doing and make sure that you're focusing your energy on that which is truly important.

3) **You'll limit the amount of willpower you have to muster.** Your willpower is a limited resource. Planning ahead of time gives your subconscious mind a sense of direction. When this happens, you don't have to think much about what you need to do next. Your behavior becomes automated, which means that you don't have to use willpower to motivate yourself before each and every task.

4) **You'll be able build momentum.** Once you complete your first task in the morning, you'll feel a sense of accomplishment and relief that builds momentum for the rest of the day. This sense of momentum compels you to accomplish more throughout the day and creates an effortless source of motivation.

5) **Your self-esteem will increase.** Many people fail to realize that self-esteem is linked to discipline. The more you discipline yourself to do what you know you should, the better your self-esteem will be.

6) **Your productivity levels will soar.** Completing your most important tasks first and focusing on one thing at a time will greatly increase your productivity.

7) **You'll experience less stress.** Planning ahead and knowing exactly what you'll have to do each day will bring you peace of mind. It will also decrease the amount of uncertainty you'll experience throughout the

day. All you need to do is look at your to-do list and complete each item one-by-one. It doesn't require much thinking and you won't become overwhelmed by all the things you need to do.

How to Plan your Day

 Things rarely get stuck because of lack of time. They get stuck because the doing of them has not been defined.

— DAVID ALLEN, AUTHOR OF GETTING THINGS DONE

Before going to bed at night, make a list of 3 to 5 tasks that will help you move towards your one thing. Now look at that list and ask yourself the following questions: If I could only accomplish one thing on this list, what would it be? Which one would have the greatest impact?

Make a commitment to complete whichever task you choose first thing in the morning, and repeat the same process for each item on your list. Don't check your emails, read the newspaper, or watch television. Avoid anything that could distract you until you've finished at least two of the most important things on your list. Remember, your ability to tackle your most important task first without succumbing to procrastination will be key in determining your level of productivity.

4 Techniques to Supercharge Your Productivity

In this section I'll provide you with several techniques that will allow you to significantly boost your productivity.

1) Using a Time Log

I'm a firm believer in the power of self-awareness. Do you want to know if you're as productive as you think you are? If so, record everything you do for a few days. Then see how much time was spent on your important tasks. You might be shocked to learn that you aren't as productive as you thought! For more on time logging, check out the following article:

http://www.stevepavlina.com/blog/2005/03/triple-your-personal-productivity/.

2) Working in Blocks

Working in blocks is a great way to stay on task and maintain your productivity. All you have to do is adjust to working on things in specific chunks of time. For optimal results, try 90-Minute Blocks, the Pomodoro Technique, or the 52/17 Method. If you're not familiar with any of these, that's okay, keep reading for a detailed description of each system.

A. 90-Minute Blocks

Implementing this method involves devoting 90 minutes to your most important tasks. Treat those 90 minutes as sacred: no interruptions allowed. Don't eat, don't drink. Don't go to the bathroom (unless you *really* need to). Don't check your emails, look at your phone, or watch TV. Focus! It's helpful to declutter your space before the 90-minute block. Clutter breeds distractions, and a clean space makes it easier to concentrate.

After the 90 minutes is up, take a 15, 20, or 30-minute break to clear your mind. It's best to completely disconnect from whatever you were working on. Spend your break doing something that refreshes you. This could mean going for a walk, reading a book, meditating, or taking a nap. It all depends on what relaxes you.

B. The 52/17 Method

Although it may seem random, recent studies have shown that employees who take 17-minute breaks for every 52 minutes of work are the most productive. It's uncertain just why this makes them more productive, but that doesn't mean you can't use this mysterious ratio to increase your own productivity.

C. The Pomodoro Technique

This method entails working on tasks in 20-minute sessions punctuated by 5-minute breaks. After four 20-minute sessions you can stretch your breaks up to 15, 20, or 30 minutes.

Choosing the Right Block Method

By now you might be wondering which technique is best. Well, that all depends. Everyone is different, so it's up to you to try them out and tweak the timeframes until you find what suits you. I tend to prefer spending at least one hour on a task before I take a break, and 90 minutes is my sweet spot.

That said, some techniques are better than others when it comes to specific tasks. With that in mind, consider the following recommendations:

- For tasks that require a lot of concentration and focus, try 90-Minute Blocks. If, for instance, you want to write an article, it's best to spend at least 90 minutes working on it before you take a break. Shorter amounts of time have the potential to disrupt your flow and increase the amount of time it takes to finish your task.
- If the task at hand will take roughly an hour complete, the 52/17 Method is your best bet.
- For tasks that don't require much concentration or creativity, the Pomodoro Technique is best. According to Robin Sharma, it takes 21 minutes to refocus after you've been distracted. As such, the Pomodoro Technique is best used for repetitive tasks that aren't mentally taxing.

You don't need to follow these techniques to the letter. The point is getting yourself to fully focus on a task without any distractions. You need to avoid multitasking at all costs, so do whatever boosts your concentration the most.

3) Dedicating a Full Day to Your Main Task

For some projects, it's more effective to spend a whole day working on them. Let's say you're a blogger who needs to shoot some videos. It would be more efficient to spend a day on that than it would be to shoot videos here and there. By devoting a whole day to it, you'll avoid the hassle of repeatedly setting up the camera and putting on your game face. You'll also be able to leverage your focus, build momentum, and complete more videos.

Some people even like to have a theme for each day of the week. Each day focuses on a different project or task. Robin Sharma is an excellent example of someone who does this. He has what he calls "creative days". On these days, he isolates himself in a distraction-free environment where he focuses solely on creative activities.

4) Visualize Your Day *

After you plan your day, take at least 5 minutes to visualize it. See yourself accomplishing everything on your list. Picture your day going exactly as you want it to. Your subconscious mind will work with those images of success while you sleep. Repeat this process the next morning before you start your day. Setting intentions is an important part of staying on track and has been proven to increase willpower.

This exercise comes courtesy of hypnotherapist Joseph Clough

From Procrastination to Action

> *Procrastination is the bad habit of putting off until the day after tomorrow what should have been done the day before yesterday.*
>
> — NAPOLEON HILL

As I've said before, the urge to procrastinate is often strongest just as we begin to work on our most important tasks. Procrastination is a huge obstacle that can seriously limit your productivity. On one hand, you're driven by fear and a powerful urge to escape. On the other, you're really passionate about you're trying to do and want to start working on it already.

The question is: how do you replace the paralysis of procrastination with action? It's not going to be easy, but the following three-step formula will help tremendously:

1. Eliminate Distractions

The first order of business is to leave as little room for distractions as possible. When you feel the urge to procrastinate, you'll find yourself interested in anything but your task. Stay one step ahead of distractions by identifying potential **procrastination patterns**. When are you wasting time and why? Is it procrastination or inefficient prioritizing that's draining your time?

Use the results of your time log investigation to create a **Not-To-Do List** based on the results you get from the time log and put the list on your desk. My list looks something like this:

- Don't check emails
- Don't check Facebook or other social media
- Don't go on YouTube or Google
- Don't go for a walk
- Don't check my phone
- Don't eat
- Don't check my book sales on Amazon
- Don't go to the convenience store to buy a drink

The next line of defense is removing all distractions from your desk. You should also plan your tasks in advance, prepare your environment, and give yourself a way to jot down intrusive thoughts. Keep phones, books, food, and other such items far away. The day before you start working on your task, spend some time visualizing yourself doing it. This will help you condition your mind and decrease the risk of distractions.

You can prepare your environment by readying the tools you'll need for your task ahead of time. Make sure everything is easily accessible. Do any and everything you can to make things as effortless as possible.

Last but not least, keep a piece of paper on hand in case something pops into your mind as you're working. Use it to write down any ideas or lightbulb moments that come to you. Otherwise, you'll remember something you forgot to do and decide to work on it... only to end up spending an hour on Facebook.

2. Become Aware of Your Fears and Emotions

- Get in touch with the feelings that come up as you gear up to work on your task.
- Be aware of your feelings when you start working on an important task
- Use a time log to bring awareness on the way you're using your time

3. Reduce the Friction Associated with Starting the Task

It's essential to reduce the discomfort involved in beginning your task. You can accomplish this through visualization. Consider your current feelings and imagine how you'll feel once your task is completed. If that doesn't work, just start and see what happens. Tell yourself you'll only work for a few minutes. You can handle almost anything for five minutes, right?

If worse comes to worst, accept the possibility that you may not do as good of a job as you'd like. Make it okay to do poorly. The reality is that you probably won't do badly unless you're extremely tired. And if you *really* think you'll do a subpar job, what makes you think you'll do any better tomorrow or next week? After all, your plan was to work on it *today*.

10

A FINAL WORD: TAKE MASSIVE ACTION

 The path to success is to take massive, determined action.

— TONY ROBBINS

Avoid the common trap of learning too much. Are you the type of person who is obsessed with learning everything they can, but don't have much to show for it? I've been there too. *But true learning can come only from doing.* You can learn all the theories and strategies you want about how to build a business, find the man or woman of your dreams, or launch a new career. But the reality is, you have no idea what you're talking about until you actually try it.

Believing that we need more knowledge is one of the most common mistakes we make. More often than not, we don't need to amass more knowledge. What we really need is to start doing something! There comes a point when we need less thought and more action. How often do we look at someone and say, "Wow, you're taking too much action! You're getting too much done"?

At best, the average person will spend one half of their time learning and the other half doing something with what they've learned. Unfortunately, that isn't enough action for those who want to make major changes in their lives. In fact, I recommend you spend at least **80% to 90%** of your time taking action. Fortunately, using a time log makes it much easier to track the percentage of time you spend taking real action.

Be honest with yourself, what percentage of your time is spent taking action towards your goals? It's time to start doing more. Why not start today? Just get going and begin building some momentum. TAKE ACTION. Action! Action! Action!

The 30-Day Challenge

To complete this challenge, engage in daily planning for the next 30 days using the 1 x 1 x 1 Rule. Start working on your primary task each day, preferably first thing in the morning, and let me know how it goes. Don't forget to put a check next to every day for which you set your daily goals, even if you don't achieve all of them!

IN CONCLUSION

It is my hope that this book gave you another perspective on productivity and will serve as a reminder of how much more you can accomplish in your life. If you implement the strategies and tactics offered here, you'll be able to significantly improve your productivity. I encourage you to refer to this book as often as possible. Look at it as a source of support as you strive to increase your productivity and establish lasting changes in your life.

You may fail many times while trying to improve your productivity. Mr. Procrastination might be lurking around every corner trying to distract you from your tasks, but that's fine. Just make sure that you make productivity a priority. Remember that the happiness of many people depends upon it, because there are people who are counting on you to provide them with something only you can give ☺.

You've made it to the end of this book so you must really like it. I really appreciate you reading this far! As a self-published author it is often really tough to market my book the way that the big publishing houses can. So, if you could take just a few minutes to **leave me an honest review,** even a brief one, I would really appreciate it.

Thanks a lot for your support!

Thanks again for purchasing this book! May you become a productive and happy person. I've included a preview of my e-book on Goal Setting at the very end of this book. Go ahead and check it out if you're interested.

Your Free ebook

Don't forget to download your Free ebook, *The 5 Commandments of Personal Development* at the following URL:

https://thibautmeurisse_1.gr8.com

What do you think?

I'd like to thank you one more time for purchasing my book. I hope you get a lot of value from it.

I'd like to ask for a small favor. Could you take a few minutes to leave a review for this book bundle on Amazon?

If you have any feedback or suggestions to improve this book bundle, feel free to send me an email at thibaut.meurisse@gmail.com

Thibaut Meurisse

Founder of whatispersonaldevelopment.org

Need some help to achieve your goals?

Hire me as a coach and I will help you achieve your goals.

More specifically we will work together to help you:

- Change your mindset and your habits
- Overcome limiting beliefs that are holding you back
- Build stronger self-esteem so that you believe in yourself and in your ability to achieve your goals
- Create an action plan and take consistent action towards your goals
- Discover your life purpose
- Stay on track with your goals long-term

To learn more contact me at thibaut.meurisse@gmail.com

Looking forward to hearing from you soon.

Thibaut Meurisse

OTHER BOOKS BY THE AUTHORS:

Goal Setting: The Ultimate Guide to Achieving Life-Changing Goals (Free Workbook Included)

Habits That Stick: The Ultimate Guide to Building Habits That Stick Once and For All (Free Workbook Included)

Master Your Emotions: A Practical Guide to Overcome Negativity and Better Manage Your Feelings (Free Workbook Included)

Productivity Beast: An Unconventional Guide to Getting Things Done (Free Workbook Included)

The Greatness Manifesto: Overcome Your Fear and Go After What You Really Want

The One Goal: Master the Art of Goal Setting, Win Your Inner Battles, and Achieve Exceptional Results (Free Workbook Included)

The Passion Manifesto: Escape the Rat Race, Uncover Your Passion and Design a Career and Life You Love (Free Workbook Included)

The Thriving Introvert: Embrace the Gift of Introversion and Live the Life You Were Meant to Live (Free Workbook Included)

Upgrade Yourself: Simple Strategies to Transform Your Mindset, Improve Your Habits and Change Your Life

Wake Up Call: How To Take Control Of Your Morning And Transform Your Life (Free Workbook Included)

Bibliography

Books

On productivity:

Getting Things Done, David Allen

On focusing:

The ONE Thing: The Surprisingly Simple Truth Behind Extraordinary Results, Gary Keller & Jay Papasan

Focal Point, Brian Tracy

On goal setting:

Goal Setting: The Ultimate Guide to Achieving Goals That Truly Excite You, Thibaut Meurisse

On valuing your time:

F.U. Money: Make As Much Money As You Damn Well Want And Life Your Life As Your Damn Well Please, Dan Lok

Videos

On productivity:

A Method To x100 Your Productivity, Robin Sharma (11mn)

On taking massive action:

Taking Action in Your Life, Project Life Mastery (8mn)

On goal setting:

How To Set Goals: The Ultimate Step-By-Step Goal Setting Workshop, Project Life Mastery (30mn)

On Procrastination:

How I Broke Free Of Procrastination, Joseph Clough (8mn)

Articles Online

Triple Your Personal Productivity, Steve Pavlina

Do a Full Day's Work in 90 Minutes, Steve Pavlina

What is Productivity?, Steve Pavlina

What Productivity Systems Won't Solve, Leo Babauta

Articles on My Blog

How to Escape the Rate Race and Live the Life you Want

7 Reasons Why You Aren't Getting The Results You Want in Life

The Recipe for Success – Are You Using The Right For Success

How To Form Habits Effortlessly – The Power Of The Compound Effect

MASTER YOUR EMOTIONS (PREVIEW)

 The mind in its own place, and in itself can make a heaven of Hell, a hell of Heaven.

— JOHN MILTON, POET.

We all experience a wild range of emotions throughout our lives. I had to admit, while writing this book, I experienced highs and lows myself. At first, I was filled with excitement and thrilled at the idea of providing people with a guide to help them understand their emotions. I imagined how readers' lives would improve as they learned to control their emotions. My motivation was high and I couldn't help but imagine how great the book would be.

Or so I thought.

After the initial excitement, the time came to sit down to write the actual book, and that's when the excitement wore off pretty quickly. Ideas that looked great in my mind suddenly felt dull. My writing seemed boring, and I felt as though I had nothing substantive or valuable to contribute.

Sitting at my desk and writing became more challenging each day. I started losing confidence. Who was I to write a book about emotions if I couldn't even master my own emotions? How ironic! I considered giving up. There are already plenty of books on the topic, so why add one more?

At the same time, I realized this book was a perfect opportunity to work on my own emotional issues. And who doesn't suffer from negative emotions from time to time? We all have highs and lows, don't we? The key is what we *do* with our lows. Are we using our emotions to grow? Are we learning something from them? Or are we beating ourselves up over them?

So, let's talk about *your* emotions now. Let me start by asking you this:

How do you feel right now?

Knowing how you feel is the first step toward taking control of your emotions. You may have spent so much time internalizing you've lost touch with your emotions. Perhaps you answered as follows: "I feel this book could be useful," or "I really feel I could learn something from this book." However, none of these answers reflect how you feel. You don't 'feel like this,' or 'feel like that,' you simply 'feel.' You don't 'feel like' this book could be useful, you 'think' this book could be useful, and that generates an emotion which makes you 'feel' excited about reading it. Feelings manifest as physical sensations in your body, not as an idea in your mind. Perhaps, the reason the word 'feel' is so often overused or misused is because we don't want to talk about our emotions. So, how do you feel now?

Why is it important to talk about emotions?

How you feel determines the quality of your life. Your emotions can make your life miserable or truly magical. That's why they are among the most important things to focus on. Your emotions color all your experiences. When you feel good, everything seems, feels, or tastes better. You also think better thoughts. Your energy levels are higher and possibilities seem limitless. Conversely, when you feel depressed, everything seems dull. You have little energy and you become unmotivated. You feel stuck in a place (mentally and physically) you don't want to be, and the future looks gloomy.

Your emotions can also act as a powerful guide. They can tell you something is wrong and allow you to make changes in your life. As such, they may be among the most powerful personal growth tools you have.

Sadly, neither your teachers nor your parents taught you how emotions work or how to control them. I find it ironic that just about anything comes with a how-to manual, while your mind doesn't. You've never received an instruction manual to teach you how your mind works and how to use it to better manage your emotions, have you? I haven't. In fact, until now, I doubt one even existed.

What you'll learn in this book

This book is the how-to manual your parents should have given you at birth. It's the instruction manual you should have received at school. In it, I'll share everything you need to know about emotions so you can overcome your fears and limitations and become the type of person you really want to be.

You'll learn what emotions are, how they are formed, and how you can use them for your personal growth. You'll also learn how to deal with negative emotions and condition your mind to create more positive emotions.

It is my sincere hope and expectation that, by the end of this book, you will have a clear understanding of what emotions are and will have all the tools you need to start taking control of them.

More specifically, this book will help you:

- Understand what emotions are and how they impact your life
- Identify negative emotions that control your life and learn to overcome them
- Change your story to take better control over your life and create a more compelling future, and
- Reprogram your mind to experience more positive emotions.

Here is a more detailed summary of what you'll learn in this book:

In **Part I**, we'll discuss what emotions are. You'll learn why you are wired to focus on negativity and what you can do to counter this effect. You'll also discover how your beliefs impinge upon your emotions. Finally, you'll learn how negative emotions work and why they are so tricky.

In **Part II**, we'll go over the things that directly impact your emotions. You'll understand the roles your body, your thoughts, your words, or your sleep, play in your life and how you can use them to change your emotions.

In **Part III**, you'll learn how emotions are formed. You'll also learn how to condition your mind to experience more positive emotions.

And finally, in **Part IV**, we'll discuss how to use your emotions as a tool for personal growth. You'll learn why you experience emotions such as fear or depression and how they work. You'll then discover how to use them to grow.

To start mastering your emotions today go to mybook.to/Master_Emotions

PART I
WHAT EMOTIONS ARE

Have you ever wondered what emotions are and what purpose they serve?

In this section, we'll discuss how your survival mechanism affects your emotions. Then, we'll explain what the 'ego' is and how it impacts your emotions. Finally, we'll discover the mechanism behind emotions and learn why negative emotions can be so hard to deal with.

1

HOW YOUR SURVIVAL MECHANISM AFFECTS YOUR EMOTIONS

Why people have a bias towards negativity

Your brain is designed for survival, which explains why you're able to read this book at this very moment. When you think about it, the probability of you being born was extremely low. For this miracle to happen, all the generations before you had to survive long enough to procreate. In their quest for survival and procreation, they must have faced death hundreds or perhaps thousands of times.

Fortunately, unlike your ancestors, you're (probably) not facing death every day. In fact, in many parts of the world, life has never been safer. Yet, your survival mechanism hasn't changed much. Your brain still scans your environment looking for potential threats.

In many ways, some parts of your brain have become obsolete. While you may not be seconds away from being eaten by a predator, your brain still gives significantly more weight to negative events than to positive ones.

Fear of rejection is one example of a bias toward negativity. In the past, being rejected from your tribe would reduce your chances of survival significantly. Therefore, you learned to look for any sign of rejection, and this became hardwired in your brain.

Nowadays, being rejected often carries little or no consequence to your long-term survival. You could be hated by the entire world and still have a job, a roof and plenty of food on the table, yet, your brain is still programmed to perceive rejection as a threat to your survival.

This is why rejection can be so painful. While you know most rejections are no big deal, you nevertheless feel the emotional pain. If you listen to your mind, you may even create a whole drama around it. You may believe you aren't worthy of love and dwell on a rejection for days or weeks. Worse still, you may become depressed as a result of this rejection.

In fact, one single criticism can often outweigh hundreds of positive ones. That's why, an author with fifty 5-star reviews, is likely to feel terrible when they receive a single 1-star review. While the author understands the 1-star review isn't a threat to her survival, her authorial brain doesn't. It likely interprets the negative review as a threat to her ego which triggers an emotional reaction.

The fear of rejection can also lead you to over-dramatize events. If your boss criticized you at work, your brain may see the event as a threat and you now think, "What if I'm fired? What if I can't find a job quickly enough and my wife leaves me? What about my kids? What if I can't see them again?" While you are fortunate to have such an effective survival mechanism, it is also your responsibility to separate real threats from imaginary ones. If you don't, you'll experience unnecessary pain and worry that will negatively impact the quality of your life. To overcome this bias towards negativity, you must reprogram your mind. One of a human being's greatest powers is our ability to use our thoughts to shape our reality and interpret events in a more empowering way. This book will teach you how to do this.

Why your brain's job isn't to make you happy

Your brain's primary job is not to make you happy, but to ensure your survival. Thus, if you want to be happy, you must take control of your emotions rather than hoping you'll be happy because it's your natural state. In the following section, we'll discuss what happiness is and how it works.

How dopamine can mess with your happiness

Dopamine is a neurotransmitter which, among other functions, plays a major role in rewarding certain behaviors. When dopamine is released into specific areas of your brain—the pleasure centers—you get a high. This is what happens during exercise, when you gamble, have sex, or eat great food.

One of the roles of dopamine is to ensure you look for food so you don't die of starvation, and you search for a mate so you can reproduce. Without dopamine, our species would likely be extinct by now. It's a pretty good thing, right?

Well, yes and no. In today's world, this reward system is, in many cases, obsolete. While in the past, dopamine was linked to our survival instinct, The release of dopamine can now be generated artificially. A great example of this effect is social media, which uses psychology to suck as much time as possible out of your life. Have you noticed all these notifications that pop up constantly? They're used to trigger a release of dopamine so you stay connected, and the longer you stay connected, the more money the services make. Watching pornography or gambling also leads to a release a dopamine which can make these activities highly addictive.

Fortunately, we don't need to act each time our brain releases dopamine. For instance, we don't need to constantly check our Facebook newsfeeds just because it gives us a pleasurable shot of dopamine.

Today's society is selling a version of happiness that can make us *un*happy. We've become addicted to dopamine largely because of marketers who have found effective ways to exploit our brains. We receive multiple shots of dopamine throughout the day and we love it. But is that the same thing as happiness?

Worse than that, dopamine can create real addictions with severe consequences on our health. Research conducted at Tulane University showed that, when given permission to self-stimulate their pleasure center, participants did it an average of forty times per minute. They chose the stimulation of their pleasure center over food, even refusing to eat when hungry!

Korean, Lee Seung Seop is an extreme case of this syndrome. In 2005, Mr Seop died after playing a video game for fifty-eight hours straight with very little food or water, and no sleep. The subsequent investigation concluded the cause of death was heart failure induced by exhaustion and dehydration. He was only twenty-eight years old.

To take control of your emotions, it is essential you understand the role dopamine plays and how it affects your happiness. Are you addicted to your phone? Are you glued to your TV? Or maybe you spend too much time playing video games. Most of us are addicted to something. For some people it's obvious, but for others, it's more subtle. For instance, you could be addicted to thinking. To better control your emotions, it is important to shed the light on your addictions as they can rob you of your happiness.

The 'one day I will' myth

Do you believe that one day you will achieve your dream and finally be happy? This is unlikely to happen. You may (and I hope you will) achieve your dream, but you won't live 'happily ever after.' This is just another trick your mind plays on you.

Your mind quickly acclimates to new situations, which is probably the result of evolution and our need to adapt continually in order to survive and reproduce. This is also probably why the new car or house you want will only make you happy for a while. Once the initial excitement wears off, you'll move on to crave the next exciting thing. This phenomenon is known as 'hedonic adaptation.'

How hedonic adaptation works

Let me share an interesting study that will likely change the way you see happiness. This study, which was conducted on lottery winners and paraplegics, was extremely eye-opening for me. Conducted in 1978, the investigation evaluated how winning the lottery or becoming a paraplegic influence happiness:

The study found that one year after the event, both groups were just as happy as they were beforehand. Yes, just as happy (or unhappy). You can find more about it by watching Dan Gilbert's Ted Talk, The Surprising Science of Happiness.

Perhaps you believe that you'll be happy once you've 'made it.' But, as the above study on happiness shows, this is simply not true. No matter what happens to you, you'll revert back to your predetermined level of happiness once you've adapted to the new event. This is how your mind works.

Does that mean you can't be happier than you are right now? No. What it means is that, in the long run, external events have very little impact upon your level of happiness.

In fact, according to Sonja Lyubomirsky, author of *The How of Happiness*, fifty percent of our happiness is determined by genetics, forty percent by internal factors, and only ten percent by external factors. These external factors include such things as whether we're single or married, rich or poor, and similar social influences.

This suggests, only ten percent of your happiness is linked to external factors, which is probably way less than you thought. The bottom line is this: Your attitude towards life influences your happiness, not what happens to you.

By now, you understand how your survival mechanism impacts negatively your emotions and prevent you from experiencing more joy and happiness in your life. In the next segment/section we'll learn about the ego.

To read more visit mybook.to/Master_Emotions

www.ingramcontent.com/pod-product-compliance
Lightning Source LLC
Chambersburg PA
CBHW071019240526
45469CB00006BD/1992